Dirty Fighting

By

Andy Puzyr

Edited by Larry Combs

Illustrations By: Bob Husth
Shelby Ward

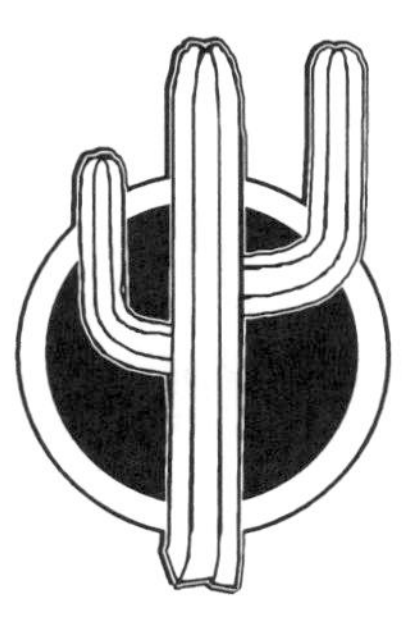

Desert Publications
El Dorado, AR 71731-1751 U. S. A.

Dirty Fighting

by

Andy Puzyr

Published by Desert Publications
215 S. Washington Ave.
El Dorado, AR 71730 U. S. A.
1-800-852-4445
info@deltapress.com
Printed in U. S. A

ISBN: 087947-071-2
10 9 8 7 6 5 4 3
Desert Publication is a division of
The DELTA GROUP, Ltd.
Direct all inquiries & orders to the above address.

Warning!!

The Publisher (Desert Publications) produces this book for informational purposes and under no circumstances advises, encourages or approves of use of this material in any manner.

Table of Contents

Contents

Dedication

I dedicate this book to my parents, whose endless sacrifices of both time and money allowed me to begin taking Judo lessons at an early age. My love of the sport provided me with the incentive I needed to explore, study, and question many other martial arts. The result of my explorations, studies, and questioning is this book.

May God be praised.

ACKNOWLEDGMENTS

I wish to take a brief moment to express my sincere thanks to the many adversaries, whose names have long been forgotten or never known, for experiencing many of the techniques described in ***Dirty Fighting***. They unwillingly provided the agonizing proof needed to substantiate the various array of theories and principles described in this book.

INTRODUCTION

My reasons for writing a book on dirty fighting are numerous. In fact, my reasons for writing are probably one of yours for purchasing...

* You've realized that much of the formal self defense you've learned just doesn't work.

* You would rather use your brains than brawn.

* You don't have a lot of time to devote towards an extensive training regime.

* You don't like to waste time; you want the fight over as soon as possible. You see no reason to sweat up a storm.

* You're not as quick or strong as you used to be.

* You simply wish to build up your arsenal of fighting "tools".

* Or you're just curious.

Whatever the reason, this book is for you!

The techniques presented in this book teach you no honorary bowing before the fight, there is no "put up your dukes", and there is no "let's go outside and settle this like men".

You are not going to learn twenty different punches and twenty different kicks to defend yourself.

The purpose of this book is teach you to defend yourself by attacking your opponent using deception and surprise, accompanied by a handful of highly effective and unconventional fighting techniques requiring a minimal amount of strength.

Finally, this is not a self defense "system". There is no fixed method of how a technique should or should not be done. If it works, use it. Anything goes.

That's right! A nice big one! Think about it, what would you do if someone flicked a huge green one at you? First you would be shocked, then you would frantically try to brush it off with your hands, as you endlessly searched where it went.

So while your opponent's hands are busy flailing, and his eyes are busy trying to locate the huge ball of mucous, deliver a swift kick to the groin.

Not only have you *physically* disrupted his defenses, but you have *psychologically* disrupted them as well. His mental preoccupation with the nasty booger has forced his concentration on it, rather than on you!

Whether you have collected a week's supply of boogies or not, you must at least *act* like you've picked one and flicked it at him.

An additional "plus" of this technique is that it brings your hands up to approximately the same level as your opponent's eyes where a finger jab can easily be executed.

The Boogie Man Reigns!

Application: As you're walking down the street, minding your own business, you notice this strange guy standing in a doorway. He doesn't look like he lives there, and experience tells you that "trouble" is on its way. Unfortunately, since there's a group of seedy characters hanging out on the **other** side of the street, crossing it to avoid any conflict is out of the question.

Begin picking your nose, digging for a HUGE nugget. If you play it up as though it's a real effort, you may even disgust your would-be assailant enough to change his mind on attacking you. If he steps out and approaches you, demanding that you hand over your wallet, flick the boogie at him. Immediately following his reaction, deliver a quick kick to the groin or a finger flick to his eyes.

I'll Do the Picking!

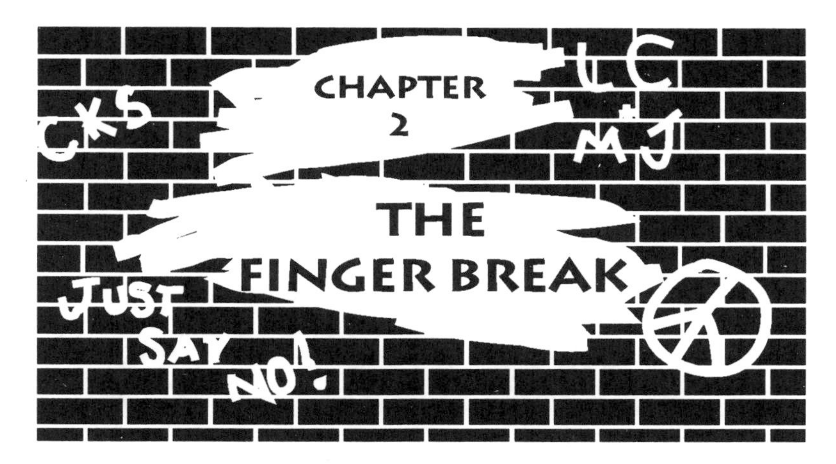

Breaking your opponent's finger is another dirty trick which not only requires very little strength, but is extremely effective in both disabling and humiliating your opponent. For now your overly-confident attacker is no longer able to grab or even make a fist to strike you. This "added feature" is very helpful should you wish to escape or apply additional dirty fighting techniques.

The Finger Break is best applied against the little (pinky) finger(s), an area *no one* is capable of resisting. However, any of the fingers could be a target, with the one exclusion being the thumb. After all, you might be up against some drug-induced weight lifter on steroids with a thumb capable of raising a car.

The Finger Break is applied by firmly grasping the pinky finger and violently jerking it backwards, against the natural movement of the joint.

The finger break is very versatile and may be applied in almost any situation. This is primarily

Please!! Gimme a Break!!

due to the simple fact that your assailant (by definition) will probably have to reach out, at one point or another, and grab you in order to prevent your easy escape. This may be when your opponent has grabbed you from the rear, underneath your arms; it may be when your opponent has grabbed you from the front, on a piece of clothing (ex: lapel, collar, etc.); or your opponent has attempted to choke you using only his hands (from either the front or rear).

Application #1: You are a woman at the movies when some Don Juan on the right of you places his left hand on your knee. Slowly place your right hand on top of his, and smile. Begin caressing one of his fingers in a sensuous manner. As Mr. Juan begins fantasizing about what the future holds, suddenly and firmly grasp the finger and snap it backwards...releasing him from his dream and into your nightmare.

Application #2: You're driving through the mall parking lot, when you suddenly see a parking space open up. You turn on your blinker and wait for the person to exit. As you pull in, you notice another guy trying to beat you to it with his hot Camaro. Naturally, your tiny '66 Volkswagon Bug beats him to it and the dude starts going berserk, laying on his horn and screaming obscenities through his T-top. As you get out, he flings open his door and rushes towards you. He begins poking you in the chest with his index finger, and accusing you of taking his spot. You apologize and try to go on your way, but no luck, this bozo wants to start something. To comply, you spit in his face and immediately grab his index finger and snap it backwards. As he thrusts his pelvis forward to relieve some of the pressure from the finger being bent back, complement the pelvis movement by executing a swift kick to his groin. One last thing, if you proceed to execute additional follow-up techniques such as slapping his ears as he drops, or grabbing his hair so you can ram his skull into a '67 Cadillac bumper; don't forget to move your car to another parking spot when you're done. You wouldn't want to come back out of the mall to see all your windows smashed and your tires flattened.

That's the Breaks!

This is similar to the Boogie Flick where the opponent is suddenly concerned with the problem of having something foreign on him which he desperately wants to get rid of.

If the drink is thrown into the opponent's face, their hands automatically come up to provide protection... leaving the groin wide open for a nice swift quick.

If the drink is thrown at the opponent's chest, the opponent's arms will probably extend out to the side as he looks down to admire the ugly mess... leaving the face wide open for a finger jab to the eyes.

Your goal is to upset the opponent's concentration. If this is done effectively, the follow-up blow is a cinch.

If you are carrying a can of soda or bottle of beer, where it is difficult to create a wide-range splash effect, then simply throw the whole can or bottle at your opponent. Some of the contents will most likely

This Round is on You!!

spill out, but remember your only goal is simply to create a distraction. Improvise.

Throwing a drink in the opponent's face is ideal if your drink has alcohol in it; for the eyes will surely get a "taste" of it. If you happen to be guzzling a drink of high proof, a quick "flick of your Bic" butane lighter will turn your opponent into a human torch. (You got to be pretty dirty for this one).

Application: Some punk wants to cut in line at your local circus to ride the Ferris Wheel. He is real obnoxious and starts blurting at profanities in front of the children. Quickly take your cup of freshly squeezed lemonade and throw it into his eyes. You know what it's like to get a squirt from an orange in your eye; can you imagine a whole cup of lemonade?! You may want to finish this ill-mannered punk off with a groin kick, but then he wouldn't be able to go on the Pony Rides.

Who buys the next round?

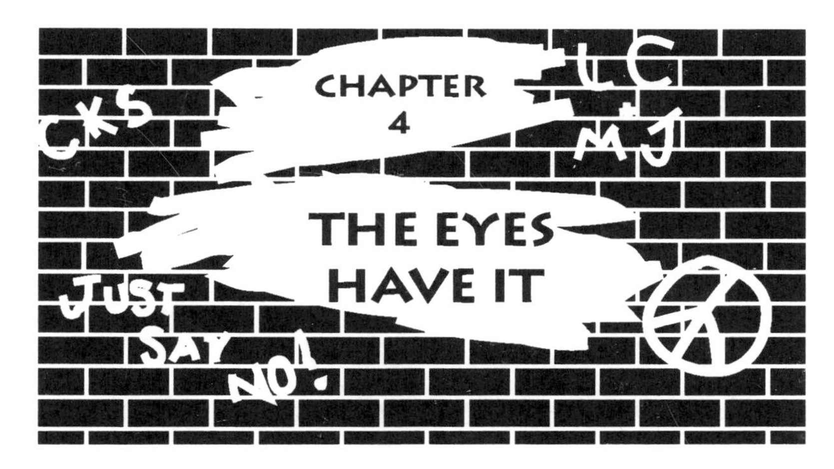

Ever get a speck of dust in your eye? Kind of incapacitating, isn't it? You can't see anything, your eyes start watering, and you just want to get the #%$&@* thing out!

That is why you should never be intimidated by an opponent's size. Think how you would feel if you were playing with a child and they accidentally stuck the point of a pencil in your eye. Even though you could easily defeat the child "in the ring", all your fighting incentive has instantly been removed, replaced now by intense pain.

Snapping out your extended fingers into an opponent's eyes is the most highly-effective technique for taking the "fight" out of them. This snapping action could also be considered a "flick"; for the action is very light. There is no follow-through motion, and the action is not a poke (as seen in The Three Stooges).

No matter who your opponent is, how much training they've had, or how much muscle they've built up, the eyes offer no (substantial) protection against a finger jab.

One major advantage of attacking the eyes is that the technique can be performed while you are off balance or are in poor position to execute another dirty fighting technique requiring more solid footing. Scratching your opponent's eyes can be done with absolutely no threat to your own equilibrium, because no real power is needed to launch it. The key element is **SPEED**.

Also, because the eyes are such a small target, **ACCURACY** is another important element. Hence... This is one technique worth practicing over and over.

See Practicing Suggestions:

One last comment; if your opponent is wearing glasses, then punch (don't flick) right through them or claw down from the top to get underneath, pulling the glasses off as you scrape his eyes.

Application: You're driving your kid down to the local hamburger joint when some moron in front of you decides to slam on his brakes because he missed his turn. You try to slow down in time, but end up "tapping" Mr. Moron's bumper. You exit your car to apologize and exchange credentials. Everything is going fine when all of a sudden, Mr. Moron notices that his vanity license plate has been bent. He immediately goes into a rampage and threatens to kill you. As he reaches towards you with both his arms, snap out your hand in between his arms and execute a finger flick to his eyes. As he releases his grip to cover his eyes, kick him in the groin. Drive away.

The Evil Eye

Eyech!!!

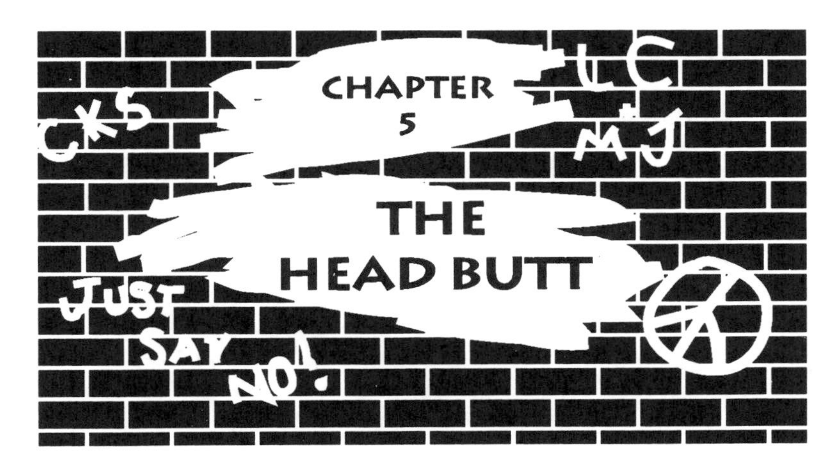

Here is one you seldom see, except of course, in Professional Wrestling.

The head butt consists mainly of snapping your head into your opponent's head. The striking area, for a frontal attack, should be your forehead aimed at the opponent's nose or teeth; for a rear attack, the striking area should be the upper-back area of your skull (above the ears) against the opponent's nose. In addition, if it is a frontal attack, your hands may or may not be used to grasp behind your opponent's neck to pull his head into yours for greater effect. If this sounds like it will hurt, it will; but not as much as it will hurt your opponent, because you are physiologically and psychologically prepared for it.

The head butt is most often applied when your opponent has grabbed you from either the front or the rear (either over or underneath your arms). The best target is the nose, not only because of its low pain threshold, but because a sharp blow to the nose will cause the eyes to instantly begin tearing. The watery

Still No "Ifs" and "Ands"!

eyes will naturally prevent your opponent from clearly seeing any further techniques launched against him.

Immediately after executing the head butt, you will notice that your opponent's grip has loosened somewhat. Take advantage of this to either get away or apply another dirty fighting trick like the knee to the groin.

If your opponent has grabbed you from behind, stomping down on his instep, breaking his finger, or quickly bending your leg which would place your heel into his groin is another follow-up technique.

Application: You are a woman playing volleyball at the beach with some of your girlfriends, when all of a sudden, some big geek grabs you from the front and attempts to carry you off to his sand castle. Snap your pretty little head right down onto the bridge of his nose. If he doesn't let go, do it again. As soon as he drops you, kick him in the groin. Encourage your friends to stomp on him as you recover from this horrible trauma.

Butt Out!!

Punching the opponent's throat can be extremely frightening (for them, not you). The pain they will experience will be nothing compared to the shocking reality of being unable to breathe. Not only will their uncontrollable fear discourage their desire to do you any more harm, but whatever they may *want* to do will be severely restricted by the lack of oxygen to the brain.

The target for this technique is the windpipe area of the throat, not the neck in general. The former will put your opponent out, the latter will just make him mad.

There are only two feasible methods for delivering a blow to the throat. One is the conventional closed fist and the other is the side of the hand (commonly referred to as the Karate Chop). The chop is more devastating due to the concentrated area making impact, but is also more difficult to apply due to the angle at which you must be to your opponent, which is either to the right or left side of him. The striking point of the chop is the area extending from the wrist to the first joint of the pinky finger.

One Gollywhopper!!

If you have a very strong grip and your opponent doesn't have a neck like a bull, you can also crush his windpipe in between your thumb and fingers. However, this area may be difficult to grab due to a high collar, heavy clothing (eg: a winter scarf), or simply an accumulation of sweat, making the area slippery. If you attempt to crush his windpipe in between your fingers, and find that you are unable to do it, do not let go without first kicking him in the groin or attacking his eyes. Otherwise, he'll become enraged that you actually tried to kill him, and may try and do the same to you.

Application: You are a woman at the movies when the same Don Juan (as before) on the right of you places his left hand on your knee. Take your left hand and place it firmly on top of his. Then quickly execute a chop with your right hand to his windpipe. The purpose of your left hand is to prevent him from raising it in protection against the chop. Note: the touching of hands will also psychologically lower his mental guard against any threat or resistance of attack (he'll think you like him).

Suggestion: If you are facing your opponent and are able to punch the throat, you are probably better off snapping out your fingers into his eyes. It is much more effective.

Warning: A serious, hard blow to the throat can be fatal, causing insufficient oxygen to the brain or large amounts of blood to fill the lungs.

Guuulp!!!

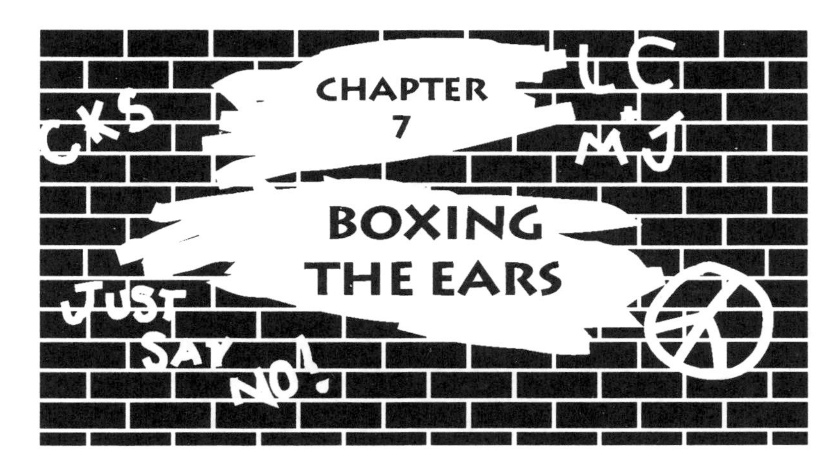

Slapping the opponent's ear or ears is extremely effective for destroying their equilibrium. Your opponent will fall to their knees, unable to stand up or even know where you are. As your opponent starts singing "Dizzy", use the time to either take off or follow-up with other dirty (or standard) fighting techniques.

The one drawback with this technique is that it is easy for your opponent to block. Thus, it is best reserved as a follow-up to a kick to the groin...where the opponent's hand-blocking defenses will be occupied elsewhere.

The ideal method of delivery for this technique is to cup the hands and strike with the palm area. Quickly take your hands away after making contact with the opponent's ears. This is to prevent them from being grabbed by your opponent as his own hands instinctly come up in response to the pain.

Slapping only **one** ear will only be half as effective. Your opponent may still retain some of their

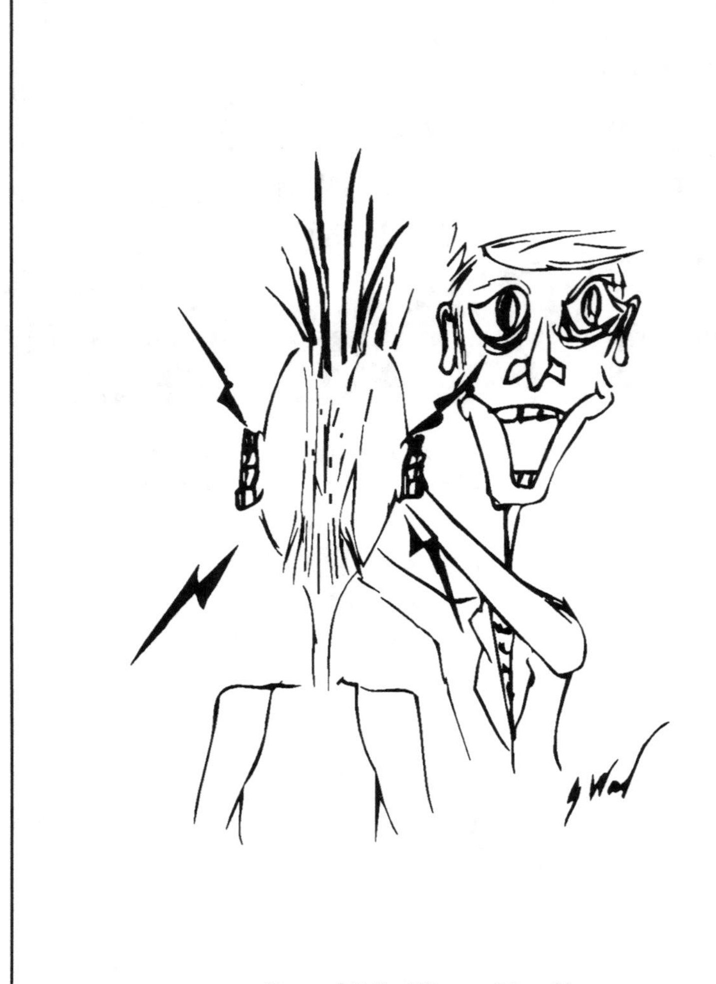

Lend Me Your Ear!!

equilibrium, thus making it possible for them to continue their attack.

This is *not* a one-shot, knockout blow, so a follow-up technique is highly recommended.

Application: You are jogging down the street when some drug freak pulls a knife and asks for your money. You assess the situation and it looks like he is going to stab you whether or not you give it to him. So "play along" and raise your hands. Then suddenly, as he is talking, spit in his eyes and immediately slap both his ears, followed by a kick to the groin.

The purpose of raising your hands is not only to have your opponent believe that you are offering no resistance, but also as a means of positioning them for greater efficiency in executing this technique.

Warning: Boxing-The-Ears can permanently damage your opponent's eardrums...as if you really care.

Heard this Before??

Biting, especially to the ears and face can be very traumatic due to its animalistic association. Not too many adversaries will continue their attack after being bitten; they'll just figure you're some kind of lunatic who's just been let out and won't want to have anything to do with you...especially if you start snarling like a cat or breathing like Darth Vader. The secret is *no words*, just snarling. Picture it!

Biting is naturally reserved for close quarters fighting, and is ideal as a surprise attack. It should be accompanied by a side-to-side, jerking movement of the head in order to generate the ripping effect similar to that of a shark.

Where to bite? Anywhere! The ears are a great target, especially if you pull away with a piece still in your mouth. This would be quite demoralizing for your opponent.

Biting is *ideal* to apply when confronted by multiple attackers. After biting the first one, the others will immediately take off, especially after seeing

HISSSSSSSSSSSSSSSSS

their friend's blood trickling down your chin. They'll have nightmares for weeks!

One last thought on biting, if your opponent looks like he is carrying some highly contagious or communicable disease (eg: AIDS, etc.), you might want to try another technique.

Application: You're a woman who's just been grabbed from the front, over both your arms, by some sleaze who not only can't take "No" for an answer, but wants to force upon you his best slobbering kiss. If you can stomach it, play along with this macho clown just long enough until he comes "within range", then suddenly take a chunk out of his nose (or one of his lips). After your opponent lets go of you, deliver the notorious (never fail) kick to the groin.

Clawing, especially if you are a woman with nails, is another excellent dirty fighting technique. What it lacks in "knockdown" power, it makes up in shock value.

The only target is the face, with extra bonus points for the eyes. It is important that clawing be followed up by a groin or knee kick, since, *alone*, it may not incapacitate your assailant.

Not unlike the finger jab, clawing can be used to attack the opponent's eyes if they are wearing glasses. Simply claw down the face, beginning from the forehead, and rip off the glasses as you scratch the eyes.

One big advantage of clawing is that it can be performed while you are not in complete control of your balance. If your assailant has surprisingly assaulted you or you happen to be standing on uneven ground, whereby resisting an attack may force you to totally lose your footing, clawing the opponent's eyes can be done with no threat to your equilibrium.

Application: Assume you're the same woman described above with the same clown trying to kiss you, but cannot possibly stomach this joker coming that near to your pretty little face. Before he has had the opportunity to grab you over your arms, or if at least one of your hands are free, claw at his eyes by attacking/reaching between and underneath his arms.

Hair pulling is an ideal method for controlling your opponent, especially if you want to drive their head into the sidewalk, a wall, or a restaurant table. I am sure you have heard the phrase "Where the head goes, the body follows". Well, it's true. Try pulling your own hair and see if you don't "go" with it.

There is not much to explain with this technique, you just grab and pull. Just remember to do something real quick after you've grabbed it, otherwise your opponent can grab hold of your arm or hand which is holding his hair and overpower you.

Hair pulling should be limited to scalp or facial hair. Pulling a guy's chest hair will only cause minor aggravation. With a woman, there usually isn't any (easily-accessible) body hair to grab other than on her scalp.

Hair pulling is a great follow-up technique after kicking someone in the groin; as they are doubled over in pain (if they have not already crumbled to the ground), grab their hair and shove their face into the pavement or nearby parking meter.

Hair pulling is also nice for pulling an opponent's head backwards (as you stand along side them) to expose their throat for a punch or chop.

Another excellent method for disabling your opponent is to pull down the hair on the back of their head with your left hand while shoving your right palm into their chin and twisting the neck in a counter-clockwise movement with both hands, as though the head were to unscrew from the spine. If your opponent has a large beard, grab the beard for greater control, rather than using just your palm. If done slowly, you will have total control over your opponent as you bring them to the ground. If done quickly, your opponent's neck will be broken. Needless to say, the "quick" method is fatal and should only be used in a life or death situation.

Application: You're sitting in the movie theater when this guy in back of you is kicking your seat, talking out loud, and being generally and purposely obnoxious. Since the movie showing is the newest James Bond flick, the movie is packed and you can't find another seat. You know that you won't get much satisfaction from the usher (who's only making the minimum wage), so you get up, turn around and politely ask him to stop kicking your seat and be a little more quiet. He blares out some stream of profanity, which you've only heard in auto repair shops, and tries to shove you back into your seat. You take advantage of his forward movement and quickly grab his hair, driving his popcorn-infested teeth into the metal backing of your seat. **Warning:** if this jackass happens to have brought a date along with him or is accompanied by some of his friends, be aware that she/they may also attack you. And since theatres are usually dark, you may not see the punch coming. If you feel you're outnumbered or overpowered, remember that fire exits aren't just for fires.

Pulling Hair Loosens Teeth!!

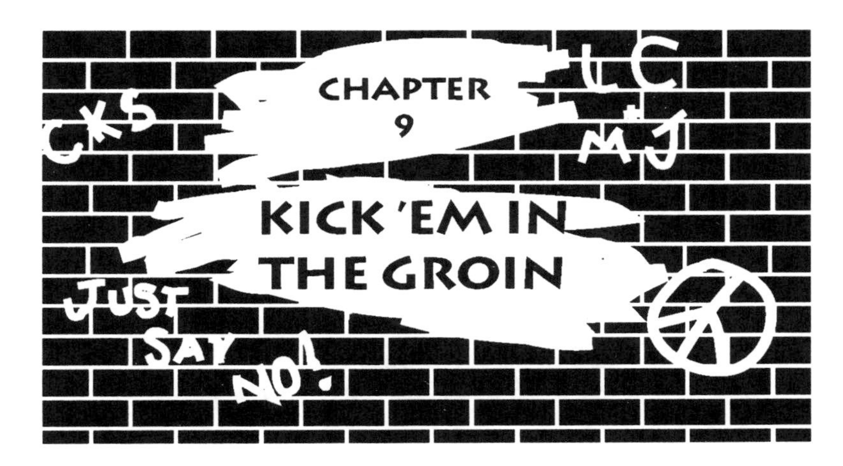

This old standby is seldom used because it is considered very dirty and hard to successfully execute. We know that it is dirty, but the reason why many people think the groin kick is difficult to successfully execute is that it is easily defended against by an experienced (male) fighter; there seems to be a "natural" defense reaction men have against it.

The key element in the groin kick's success is not to "telegraph" the kick (ex: look at the groin and then kick). C'mon, unless you have never seen another human before, you already know where the opponent's groin is, so just kick!

There is no need to generate Bruce Lee power...very little is needed.

If your attacker is a woman, a quick punch to the breast (I have been told) is equivalent to the groin kick. And you have two to choose from. *Editors Note: My informal survey among females is that they don't think that this punch is equivalent to the male groin kick.*

Punt!!!

Though the kick is specifically mentioned here, punching the groin is also effective. If Mr. Macho tells you to, "Get on your knees", (and he is close enough) his groin is an open target. Remember to punch upwards, not straight out.

An excellent method for practicing this technique is simply to aim at a target at about groin height and lightly kick it with a snap. The target could be anything, even the towel hanging from your refrigerator door. The important thing is to AIM.

After a kick to the groin, there should be no great concern that your opponent is going to quickly recover and begin chasing you down the block. The **movies** may want you to believe this great piece of fantasy, but all guys know that it is simply impossible.

Application #1: Mr. Harley approaches and accuses you of looking at his biker girlfriend. First he pokes you in the chest, then he starts with the ole' tuff-guy shoving. As his arms extend outward and his weight shifts forward, take a quick step back out of his reach. His physical and mental balance will be momentarily out of control. Instantly step forward and kick him in the groin.

Optional: As your opponent squirms on the ground, grab his girlfriend **and** bike and ride off into the sunset.

Application #2: You're sitting in a booth at a roadside truck stop, when some redneck decides he doesn't like the length of your hair. As he stands at the edge of your table and spits a huge wad of chewing tobacco in your lap, grab the plastic ketchup bottle and quickly squirt him in the face (note that ketchup contains a large amount of salt and vinegar - "great" for the eyes!). Then suddenly, execute a quick punch to his groin, which will be at a very convenient level with your fist.

I Think My Voice is Changing!

This is another variation of the Kick 'Em In The Groin technique, so it is only natural that I follow with it here.

The knee kick/lift is best applied only to the groin, and is reserved only for close frontal confrontations (either standing or lying down) where a kick with the foot would be impractical due to the close proximity of your opponent.

Since a quick lift of the knee is a very unnatural movement (unless you're a hurdler), this technique should be practiced often; for many encounters begin much too close to remain at a safe or comfortable distance. It is best to practice this technique against a low-hanging heavy bag, though you may also use your outstretched hand. Remember, accuracy against the groin is what's important, not power.

Do not use the knee kick to pull down your opponent's head, as is often seen in the movies. Not only is this technique not as easy as the movies make it seem, but you could suffer from some nasty teeth gashes in your knee from trying it.

Just a Knee-Jerk Reaction!

Application: Mr. Macho and you are standing nose-to-nose while he screams how he is going to beat you to a pulp. As he conducts this one way piece of intellectual dialogue, sharply lift up your knee into his groin. For an added effect, do it a second time...before his hands drop down to "nurse" the tender area. As he writhes over in pain, the choice is yours...you can take off, box his ears, kick him in the face, or go for ice cream.

Hint: Knee him while he is talking, while his peanut brain is occupied with trying to construct sentences... rather than occupied with defending himself.

Knee Deep in Trouble!

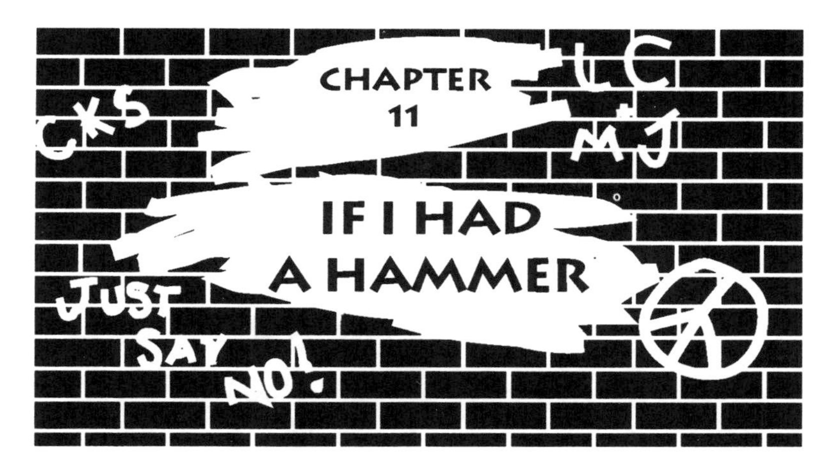

If you are a woman wearing high heels, you already have an excellent weapon right at the tip of your toes.

At the first sign of a serious confrontation, immediately get out of your heels. You won't look as good, but you'll be able to defend and attack much more effectively. As you remove your shoes, grab the toe portion and strike with the pointed heel. This will give your assailant not only a blood-spewing gash but also a headache he will never forget, **that is** unless you strike him in the temple and he lapses into a coma. And remember, do not stop hammering until the threat of further attack has been eliminated.

If your opponent raises his hands to protect his head, simply hammer elsewhere...like the groin.

The most effective targets are those which are relatively bony, such as the skull, the hands, the knees, and the instep. Softer tissues (aside from the groin) will only "help" cushion the blow, thus causing much less pain.

If the Shoe Fits!!!

Suggestion: Unless the shoes are extremely expensive Italian imports or happen to match your favorite mini skirt, leave them with your attacker as a token of your fond encounter. Walking down the street with a chunk of scalp hanging off your pump might raise some questions.

Application: You're on your way home from work, all "dolled up" but in no mood for romance. You stop at the local Burger King to pick up a quick bite to eat. As you're sitting there enjoying your large fries, a group of rowdy teenagers comes in. One eyes you up and says something to his buddies. You get the feeling that your meal won't be an entirely peaceful one. Slowly cross your legs beneath the table, bringing the foot of the crossed leg as high as possible to allow a quick grab of your pump. As suspected, the jerk that was checking you out, comes over and tries to impress his friends by "proving" that he can pick you up. Your polite refusals are returned with his hand caressing your hair. You instantly throw your milkshake into his eyes, grab the pump, and hammer the pointed heel into his forehead. (As an alternative, you can also punch him in the groin, since it will be at a very convenient level with the table and your fist).

Note that it is extremely doubtful that his friends will try and attack you, since they'll probably be laughing at their buddy covered with the milkshake, squirming on the floor. However, he may want to seek revenge on you for humiliating him in front of his friends, so make sure you drive away in a direction where your license plate can not be easily read as you pass under the parking lot lights.

Hammer Home Your Point!!

You've probably heard that the knee only requires seven pounds of force to break. Though the "break" is actually a dislocation, the seven pounds estimate is very near the truth. However, many factors are necessary for this dislocation to be successful:

First, the kick must strike at the correct angle without glancing off, otherwise the natural, springy resilience of the knee will withstand the blow.

Second, the opponent's knee must have the correct amount of body weight distributed on it, otherwise (if too little body weight) the knee will simply give or (if too much body weight, against an opponent whose legs could hold up a piano) the large muscle groups will support the knee and absorb the blow.

Third, the kick must be a kick, not a push (often) caused by the kicker leaning excessively backwards.

The kick to the knee is best executed with a snapping movement directed at a 45-90 degree angle

Kneed I say More???

to the knee (from the inside or outside) with the bottom or side of the foot (not the toe or ball). The ideal distribution of the opponent's body weight should be about equal between both legs. However, do not suffer "analysis paralysis" in calculating how much body weight is distributed. If the opportunity presents itself to kick your opponent's knee while his full body weight is on it, then go for it. You may not dislocate the knee, but you will certainly prevent him from attaining a full speed run after you should you decide to take off.

A properly executed knee kick will guarantee torn ligments and tendons for your opponent; the leg which once provided him both strength and support will now be nothing more than a wet noodle.

If you plan on sticking around (for what's left of the fight) to try some of the other techniques mentioned, you'll have a much easier and enjoyable time, since your opponent's mobility will be severely hampered.

If your kick does not thoroughly incapacitate your opponent, either kick at the same knee again, kick at the "good" knee, or use a fake kick at the injured knee as a feint for follow-up techniques.

More food for thought...

If you happen to be on the ground, kicking your opponent's knees as a means of defense is very effective. Not only will the constant kicking weaken them, but as he tries to spread his legs so you can no longer get to his knees, guess what is now a wide open target?!

Application: You're lying on the beach catching some rays, when Mr. Muscles comes along and kicks sand on your hot dog. Immediately throw your ice cold soda on his hot body to put him into a state of mild shock. Then execute a forceful kick to his leading knee (the one closest to you). After he drops to the sand along side of you, pull out your umbrella and stab him with the point. If you have some sunburn spray handy, you can use that to spray in his eyes. Let your imagination wander.

Another excellent (but more complicated and time consuming) way of delivering this technique is to take your other (non-kicking) foot and hook it behind the opponent's foot of the leg which you plan to kick. This will essentially "lock" your opponent's leg, preventing it from yielding backwards, forcing his leading knee to take the full brunt of the blow as you kick it into the next blanket.

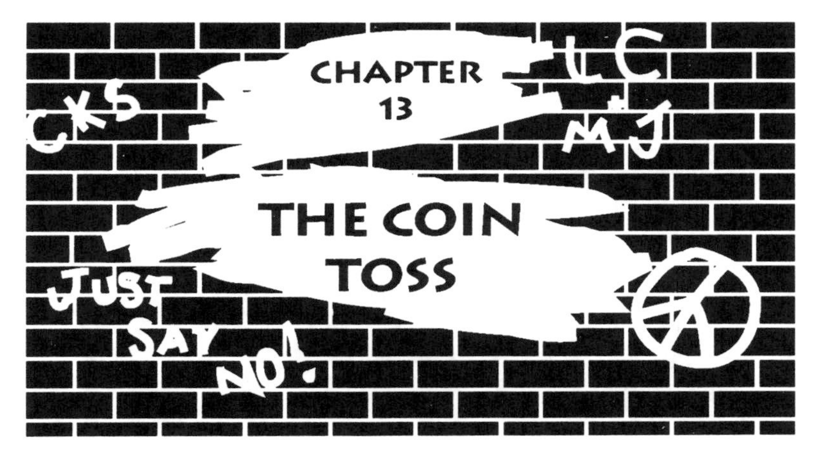

Carrying spare change in an easily accessible coat pocket and tossing it into the opponent's face is an ideal way to distract them for a sharp kick to the groin.

In fact, this technique was often practiced by the Japanese Ninja, only they would use pepper or some other irritant for greater effect.

Do not attack the opponent's eyes or head area after tossing the coins because their hands may be raised in protection from the flying coins. You would be thwarting your own attack.

An additional reason for not attacking the head area is that the opponent may have leaned too far back to avoid the coins, thus making a strike to the face impossible.

Never use your car keys to throw at your opponent. The obvious reason is that you may need them to get home; and if it's dark, you may not be able to find them. You may also need the keys to run down multiple attackers in case your opponent's friends show up to help.

It's going to be tails!

Besides coins, a few five or ten dollar bills thrown on the ground as you take off is another great distraction. If your opponent is out to rob you, well then, he got what he wanted; you've just slightly changed his plans by running away. If he's a punk out to simply rough you up, the thought of having all that cash on the ground may seem alot more appealing than sticking you with his knife. It may be more bills than you'd like to carry or throw away (for that matter), but think of it as insurance...a fraction of the cost of a night in the hospital or emergency room.

This technique is best applied in situations where you already have your hands in your pockets or have a reason to put them there (e. g. "gimmie your money"). Otherwise, your opponent may think you have a weapon and decide to charge you; and with both hands in your pockets, you're a sitting duck.

If you smoke, flicking a lit cigarette into your opponent's eyes is a great alternative to using coins. A few burning ashes singeing the cornea will stop the meanest dude in town.

Application: You just got out of work and you begin walking to the subway tunnel. It's bitter cold, so both hands are shoved deep inside your pockets. As you're standing around waiting for the subway, some punk decides he wants to rob you of your vintage WWII Flying Aces jacket (which, of course, has kept you warm through countless battles behind enemy lines). Before he pulls out a weapon, immediately toss your subway tokens, your change, and favorite nail clipper from your pocket into his face.

As he steps back and raises his arms to protect his eyes, execute a well-aimed kick to the groin. Then push him onto the tracks with the rest of the vermin.

It's Worth It!!

Pens and pencils make great stabbing weapons which can be readily accessible and naturally inconspicuous in a top shirt pocket. A pen jabbed into your opponent's eye, throat, or ear can totally ruin their whole day.

I highly recommend the cheap (once 19 cents) BIC pens constructed from a clear plastic tube. These pens are extremely strong and may be left protruding from your opponent's eye socket without any second thoughts about losing a good quality pen.

The pen should be held in the matter which will dictate its use. If your opponent is charging you from the front, hold the pen like you would normally hold a kitchen knife for cutting and thrust it into his throat or eyes. If he is sitting along side you, grasp it like an ice pick and thrust it into his leg or side of his face.

When using this technique, do not use a constant follow through motion. The attack should be more like a thrust, with an instant (snap) return of the

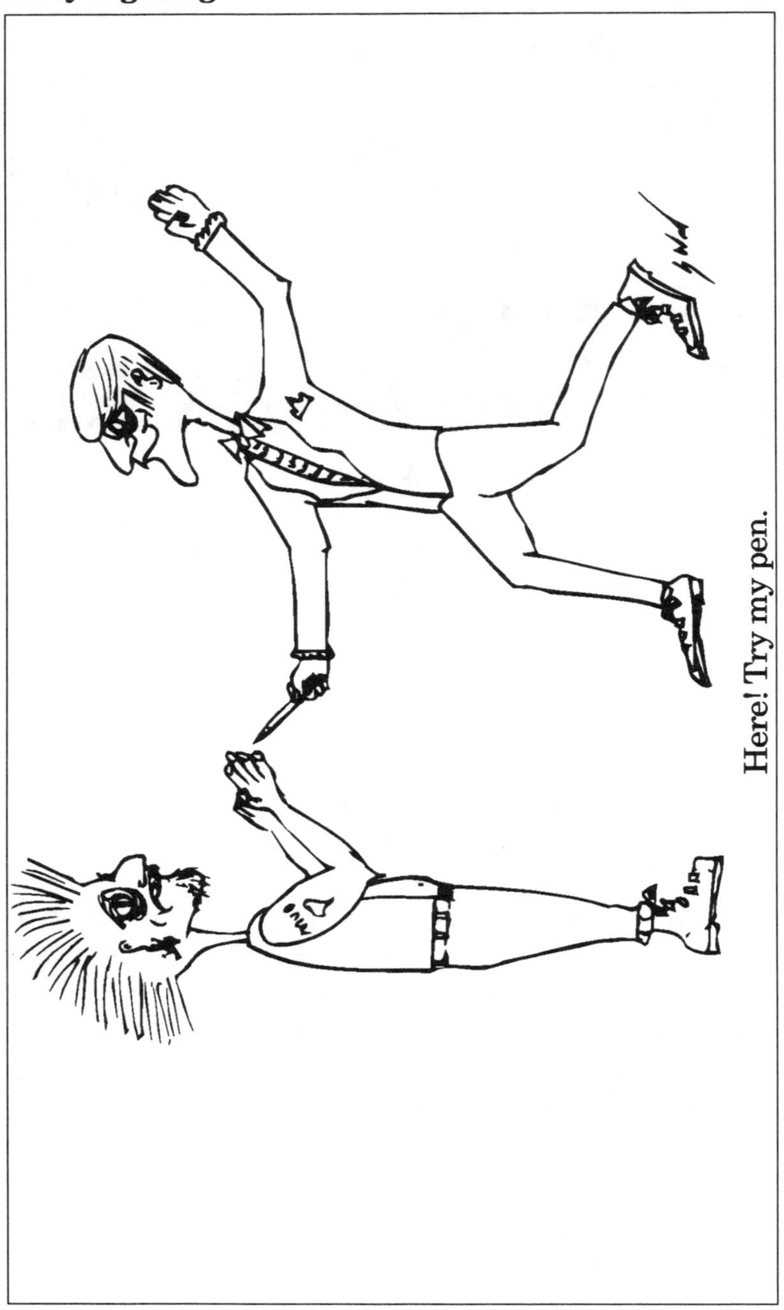

Here! Try my pen.

hand. Otherwise, as your opponent's hand naturally gravitates towards the injured area, he may grab hold of your arm and overpower you.

The pen technique which should be practiced frequently. You can even simulate various encounters like a boxer does when he shadowboxes. Concentrate on accuracy rather than raw power; with the small point of a pen, you won't find penetration to be a problem. A styrofoam head, used for mounting wigs, makes an excellent target; for you'll simultaneously get the feeling of resistance while enjoying the essence of realism.

Note: Due to the nature of felt tip pens with their soft points, avoid using them. However, if it's all you've got, then go for the eyes.

Application: You're a woman (or man) sitting alone in the theater when some jerk tries to get "lovey-dovey" with you. Be nice and tell him "No". If he shows no sign of stopping, throw your greasy popcorn into his face. Immediately grab your trusty Bic and thrust it into his thigh or groin.

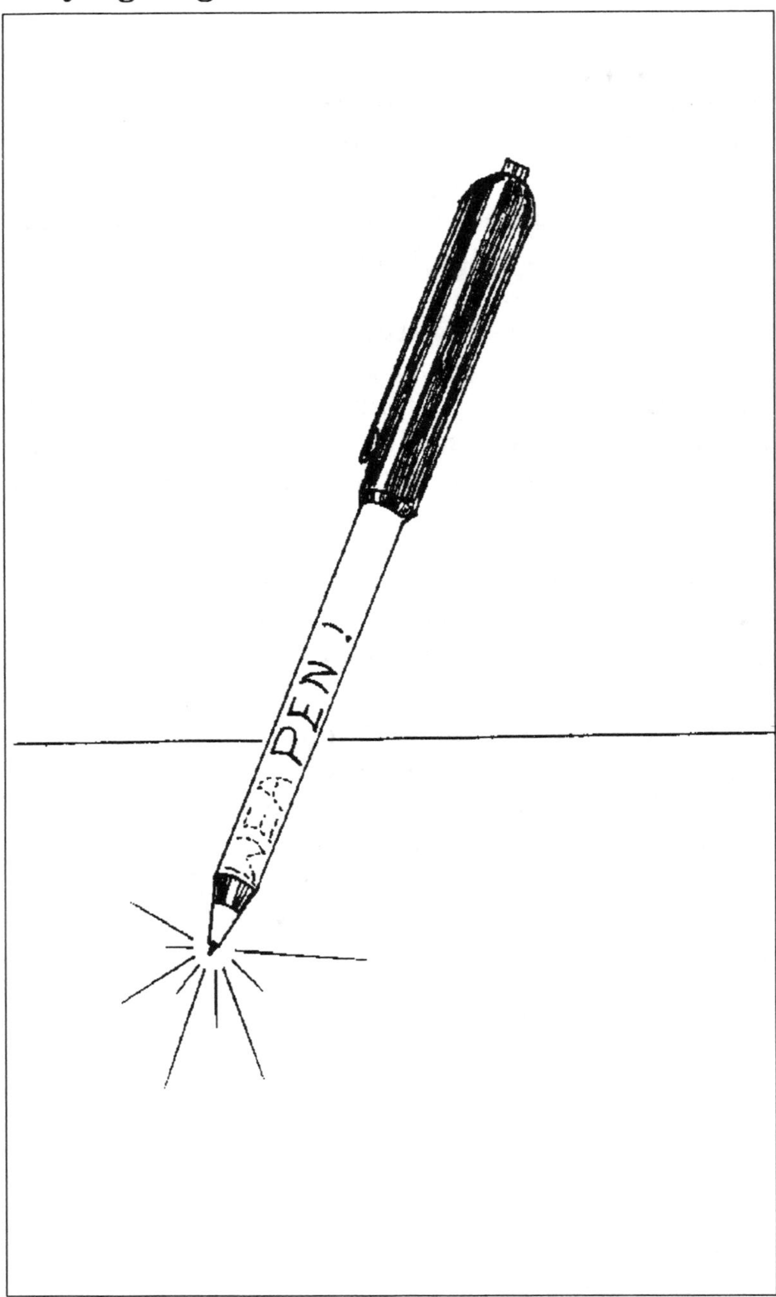
WEAPEN!

Acting timid and afraid will often cause your opponent to suddenly feel superior and assured that you are easy prey and will offer no resistance. This false sense of confidence opens the opponent up for a quick finger jab to the eyes, especially if you raise your hands slowly in front of your face and let out a truly mousy squeal of "Please don't hurt me".

Never utter just one simple plea and wait for your opponent's response. It won't be convincing. You must act like a nervous, babbling fool. Here is an example: "Oh please don't hurt me, please don't hurt me. I'll give you anything. Please don't hurt me, oh p-l-e-a-s-e don't hurt me. What do you want? Oh please don't hurt me." Convincing? Pathetic? Or both?

The situation for applying this technique requires a strong sense of being able to "read" people...along with an honest look at your self and physique. If you look like a nerd and think you can get away with this little drama, then use it. If you are built like a barn, it is doubtful your opponent will fall for the performance.

Now you wouldn't hurt me would you?

Application: The play "My Fair Lady" just let out and you and your date are on the way back to the parking deck to pick up your wheels. You're both "dressed to the hilt", giving everyone the impression that you're "made of money". With you in your rented tux and your date in her fancy gown, you both seem easy prey. Several teenage punks approach you and ask you for your wallet and your date for her purse. Now it's showtime...

With your best quivering voice, you say "Oh my, oh my! What are we gonna do? Look, I'll give you guys whatever you want. I'll give you our money, just don't hurt us. Please don't hurt us. Here's my wallet." Shakingly reach for your wallet and then immediately drop it. After you're told to pick it up (which you will be). Do so, but this time toss it straight up and high in the air, above their heads. As his/their eyes follow the wallet up, quickly kick the one closest to you in the crotch. Without hesitation, instantly kick one of the other punks (preferably the next closest to you or the one hypnotized by the flying wallet).

Suggestion: When roaming "bad" neighborhoods, always carry a spare, "throw away" wallet for situations such as this. If you've ever been robbed, you know that it's not the loss of the money which is so aggravating...but the endless grief of having to call credit card companies, banks, or even replace a driver's license. A cheap wallet with a couple of business cards and ten dollar bills stuffed inside will not only make the wallet appear genuine, but may also pacify your robber(s) to let you go on your merry way.

Oh! Pleeeese! Oh! Pleeeese! Oh! Pleeeese!

This is the greatest distraction of them all, because it is never, ever expected. The eyes automatically blink as part of their natural protection response system. When they open again, all they see is an incoming fist, eye gouge, or "stars" as they experience the excruciating pain from your groin kick.

The secret to spitting is to generate a "spray" affect versus pin point accuracy. The obvious reason is that "spraying" increases the chance of hitting your target. Practice, practice, practice.

It is important not to wait until your opponent's eyes open again before attacking. Do not hesitate. Spit and kick. The two movements should flow together.

This technique is so effective, that I would precede all my attacks with it. It requires no costly expense of energy and unless you've just completed eating a box of Saltines, saliva is always available. What better setup is there which forces your opponent to CLOSE his eyes?! Nothing could be better!

Spit! Spit! Spit! Spit! Spit!

Hint: Whatever you may have in your mouth can easily substitute for spit...whether it be gum, a breath mint, or a hamburger.

Application: You've just finished attending a night school class in Wok Wizardry. On your way back to the car, you notice some punk trying to steal the hubcaps off your '66 Ford Fairlane. As he sees you approaching, he sizes you up and becomes immediately confident that he can take you on. As you politely asked him to return the hubcaps, slowly walk towards him to get within spitting distance. While he screams his intentions of how he is going to beat the living crap out of you, spit a mouthful of saliva and bean sprouts into his eyes. Immediately follow-up with a quick kick to his crotch. Note that you may have to further follow-up with a kick to the knee or with boxing his ears (as he's holding his groin), since it's night time and you may not have had clear enough vision to execute a precise kick to his jewels.

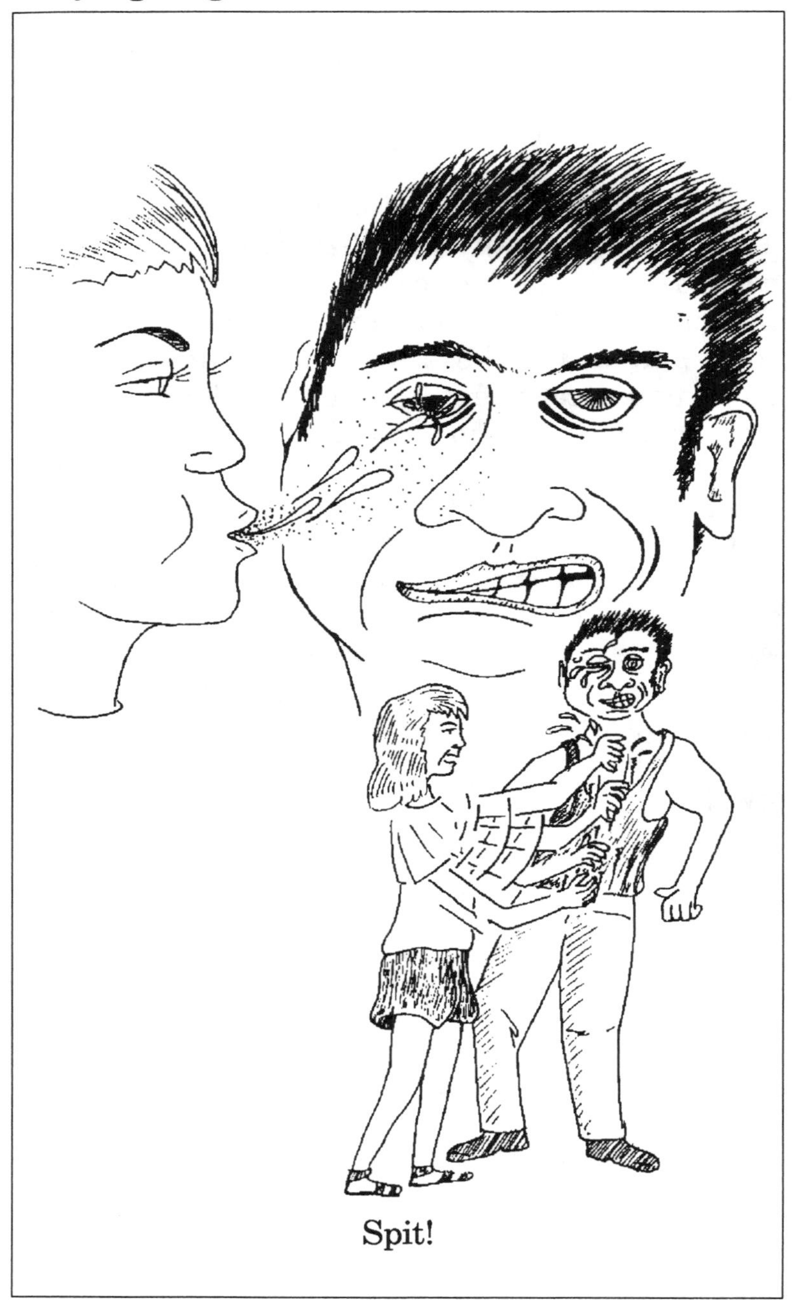

Spit!

Stomping down on the opponent's instep is an excellent technique which causes excruciating pain, providing, of course, your opponent isn't wearing steel-toed work boots with two pairs of socks.

There isn't much to explain with this technique - just lift up your foot and stomp down. The striking point should be the heel or side of your foot. Aim close to your opponent's shin.

Remember not to "telegraph" your intentions by looking down at your opponent's foot and then proceeding to step on it. As you're looking down, your opponent may decide to launch a quick punch to the side of your head.

This technique is best applied while you are standing in front of or alongside your opponent. If your opponent has grabbed you from behind, you can also apply this technique; however, it will be more difficult since you may not be able to see your opponent's feet. This technique is not recommended if you are barefoot or are wearing sneakers, since you will not be able to generate a truly debilitating blow.

Foot loose and not free!

Special hint: Once you have successfully stomped on your opponent's instep, it makes a great feint for later on. Simply slap your foot down to generate a thump and attack his eyes. Your opponent will hear the slap and will immediately associate it with pain. This bad memory acts as a distraction for your follow-up technique. I have successfully used this feint on many seasoned fighters, including black belts.

Application: You've been standing in line for hours at the Division of Motor Vehicles waiting to renew Grandma's license. As you look back to wave at sweet ole' Grandma, some big jerk cuts in line, right in front of you. You tell him that you were here first and that he has to wait his turn like everyone else (as though it's going to help). As he turns back to face you, he shoves his elbow hard into your gut. Then, to make matters worst, he blurts out a whole bunch of naughty words in front of Grandma. You notice he's wearing sandals, so you immediately drive the heel of your cowboy boot into his instep. As he drops to his knees and bends over, kick him in the face as you would punt a football. If the jerk doesn't fall to the floor (possibly because your accuracy was off), but lifts his foot and starts to hop around, grab his hair and drag him into the nearest metal desk (there are usually an abundance of these around in government offices).

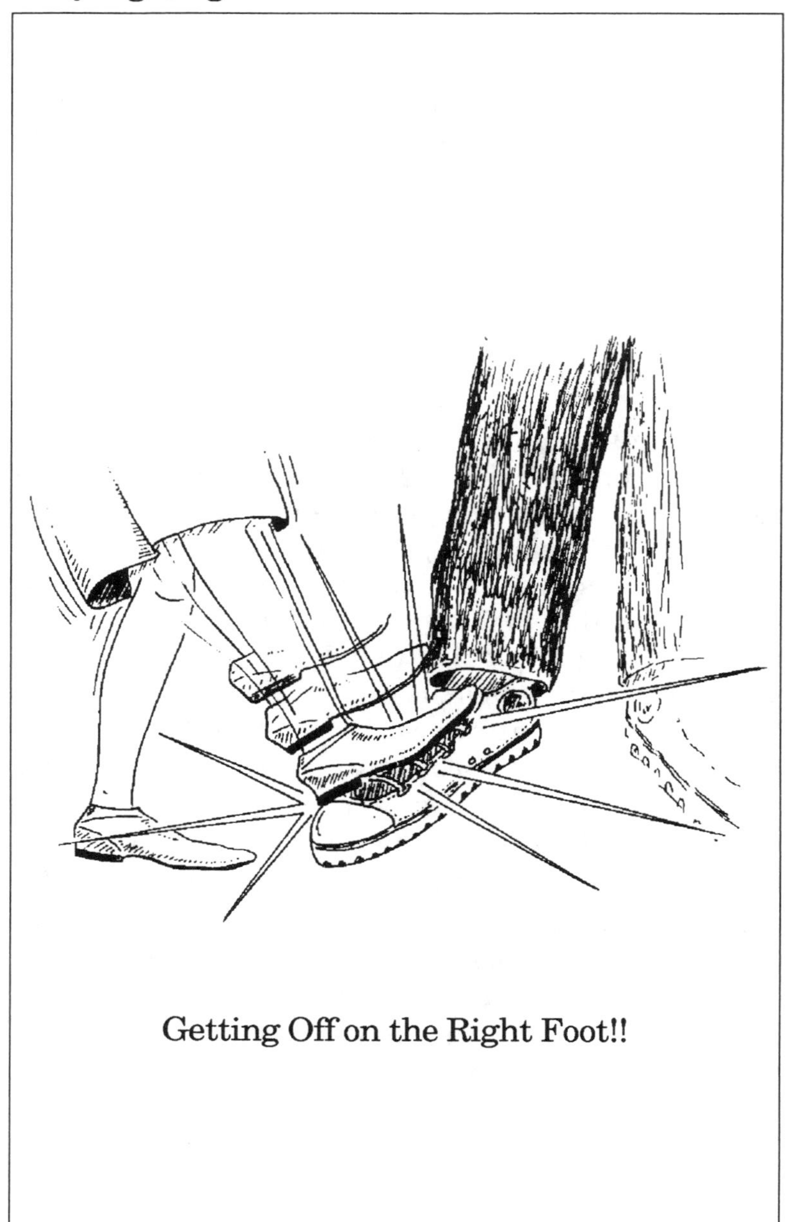

Getting Off on the Right Foot!!

This technique is often used by woman against men. Probably because women know that their legs are stronger than their arms and can do a lot more damage, and probably because their arms are too busy trying to hold back the man.

Kicking your opponent in the shins is naturally something you only want to do with hard-soled shoes. If you're barefoot, wearing sneakers, Hush Puppies, or any soft-soled shoe...forget it; you'll only end up "ticking off" your opponent! Kicking the shins is definitely not a crippling blow, but it is very effective in setting up your opponent for more devastating techniques. It is often used to lure your opponent's arms down, leaving the head area open for an attack. Sometimes kicking the shins requires more than one kick (but not necessarily to the same leg) to have an obvious effect on your opponent. But don't go "chasing" after his legs as your opponent tries to evade your kicks; if he is busy watching your kicks, try something "upstairs" - like a finger jab to the eyes.

If you're lying on the ground (either resting or as a result of a push), kicking your opponent's shins will

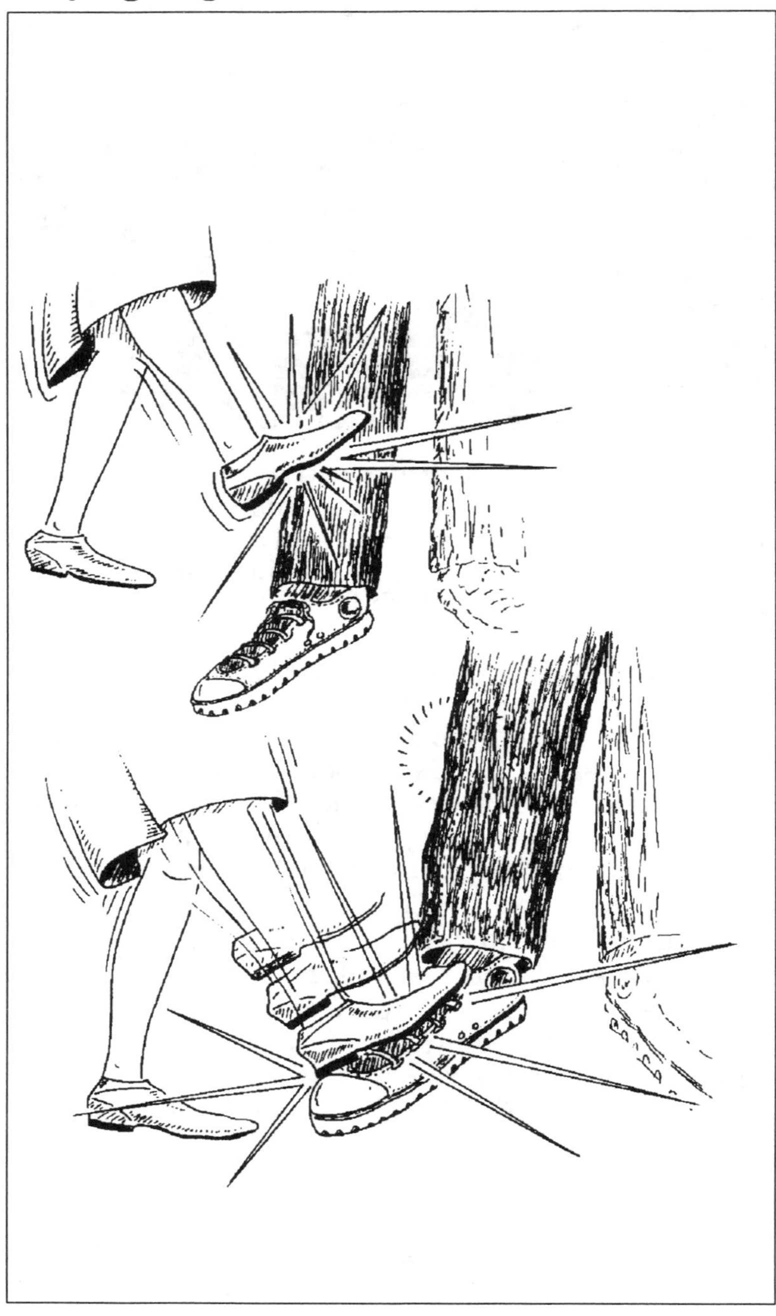

temporarily keep him at a safe distance. However, do not rely on this technique or continue with its execution over a long period of time (greater than five kicks). Otherwise, your opponent will soon be able to anticipate your kick, and subsequently grab your leg. Then you're in real trouble. See "Pop Goes The Knee".

The area you should try and strike with is the edge of your shoe, whether it be the inside or outside. Do not attempt to strike with the toe, especially if you're wearing pointed shoes; the chance of effectively hitting your opponent's shins squarely is almost nil. Conversely, if your wearing army or construction boots with a wide toe (better yet, a metal toe) then by all means, strike with the toe and give it all you've got!

Application: You're attending an outdoor Barbara Streisand concert that only has lawn seats available. As you're lying back on the grass, with a perfect view of the stage, some jackass comes along and sets up his beach umbrella right in front of you, totally blocking your wonderful view of Babs. You ask him if he would mind closing his umbrella. He utters a few choice words to the effect of "No", and then comes over and asks if you would like to "make something of it". Even from the ground, you can smell the distinct odor of Jack Daniels on his breath, so you mentally and physically prepare yourself for an encounter. Suddenly he starts kicking your feet, in order to provoke a fight. Not to deny his provocation, you swiftly kick him in the shins - preferably as he is kicking you in order to combine his forward force with your own. Since he is stinkin' drunk, he will probably fall to the ground, where you can follow-up with whatever suits your fancy. As a suggestion, go over to his umbrella; and if it's the kind that breaks apart into two pieces, remove the bottom part and beat him with it.

Believe it or not, shouting is another form of distraction which can be extraordinarily effective. In fact, it is so effective that it is taught in many of the martial arts, commonly referred to as a "kiai".

The purpose for shouting is twofold: it suddenly increases your adrenalin, thereby improving your strength and speed, while also disrupting your opponent's composure. Why do you think the American Indians used it (a.k.a. war cry) preceeding their attacks? It has great psychological advantages.

The shout should not be initiated by fear or timidly executed; the shout should be commanding and assertive. This is extremely important! Practice. Yes, practice!

As an added bonus to the shout, send a mouthful of spit along with it. This may require some doing, but your opponent won't know what's happening!

The shout is best employed when your opponent is either attacking or talking. The shout will disrupt

Words are stronger than arms!

his thought process and provide a psychological opening for an attack.

Hint: Include a psychotic, glaring stare at your opponent. The key here is psychotic (or crazed), not the plain old "determined" look as seen by boxers in the ring as they stare down their opponent. Remember that your intention is to disrupt your opponent's psyche, not compete in a "I'm tougher than you are" staring contest.

Application: You're standing in line at the concession stand at your local movie theatre. You ask the zit-invested, burn-out behind the counter for an orange drink. He gives you an orange soda. You politely correct him and ask again for an orange drink. He says, "Like wow man, you said 'soda'. What are ya, stupid or somethin'?" You refuse the soda and he forcefully slides in towards you. It spills all over your favorite cow t-shirt. Stare him squarely in the eyes and let out a quick, forceful yell. The second that he shows being startled, grab a lock of his purple-dyed hair and slam his face through the glass counter and into the Gummi Bears.

* Translation: "Stop" in Scared Language!

Do you think it's gonna rain?
What's your favorite color?

Confused? What does this crap have to do with dirty fighting?

That's just the point.

Disrupting an opponent's state of mind can not only be accomplished through physical means (spitting, body movements, eye feints, etc.), but can also be accomplished through psychological means, such as making a statement which is totally out of context.

Application: Bad Guy: Gimmie your money!
You: No.
Bad Guy: If you don't gimmie your money I'm gonna punch your lights out!
You: What about the parade?

As the Bad Guy is trying to figure out what a parade has to do with his plans of punching your lights out, his mind is momentarily preoccupied.

Space flight or fancy?

Since two thoughts cannot occupy the brain at one time (the Bad Guy analyzing your remark while simultaneously remembering his intentions of robbing you), take advantage of this psychological distraction to kick him in the groin.

Whatever verbal response you make, it is better to phrase it into a question rather than a simple statement. A question requires more of a thought process from your opponent, which translates into additional time to launch your attack. But don't become overly-confident...this state of confusion within your opponent's mind is very short; do not hesitate in attacking. Speak and kick.

Watch your opponent's eyes; they will often reveal a sense of puzzlement.

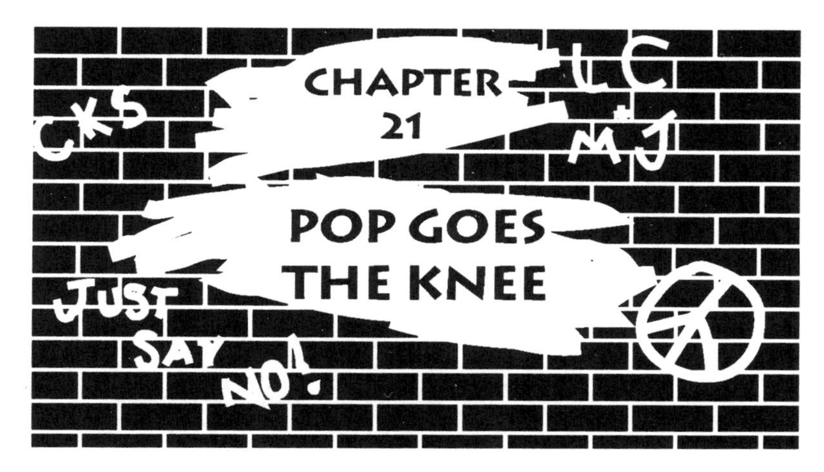

If your opponent is a high kicker (above the waist), and you have the opportunity to grab his leg, maintain your hold of it and immediately kick out the knee of his supporting leg. Do not kick behind his knee so it just bends and he collapses to the ground. You must kick the knee at a 45-90 degree angle so the joint is totally demolished.

Hint: Watch out for your opponent's fists, he may have long arms and "clock" you one as you come in.

If your opponent has long arms and long legs, it will be difficult to kick out his supporting knee without getting punched in the process. So, once you've grabbed his kicking leg, maintain hold of it and "inch" your way out to his foot. When you've reached the foot, violently jerk it towards you and to his outside (his left foot is twisted to your right while his right foot is twisted to your left). The successful execution of this technique will dislocate your opponent's knee with a sickening "pop".

If you fail to violently jerk and pull the foot, you will only hear the tearing cartilage and ligaments...no

SNAP!
CRACK!
POP!

"pop". But the effect will undoubtedly be the same...non-stop screaming.

Application: You're about to enter Dominick's Pizza Shop when a small group of teenage boys loitering outside decide to block the doorway. Since you're in a hurry to pick up your pie, you don't feel like exchanging alot of "macho" dialogue. You tell the one who is blocking the door to get out of your way. He refuses and shoves you backwards. He assumes some kind of crazy Kung Fu stance and attempts to kick you in the chest. You instantly grab his kicking leg and forcefully kick out his supporting knee with a quick snap of your foot. If one of his friends tries to join in, and this you should be on the lookout for, ram their head through the large storefront window (which most pizza shops have so you can watch' em flip the dough).

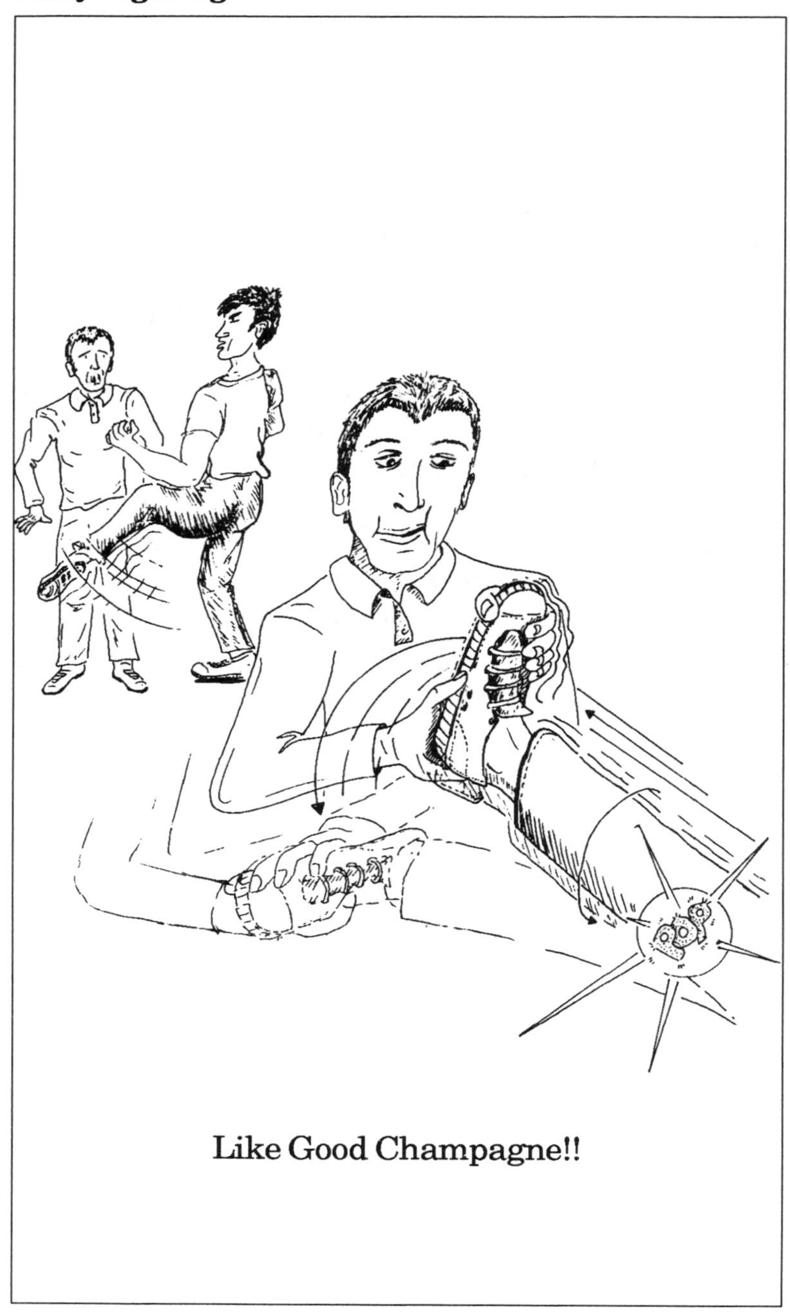

Like Good Champagne!!

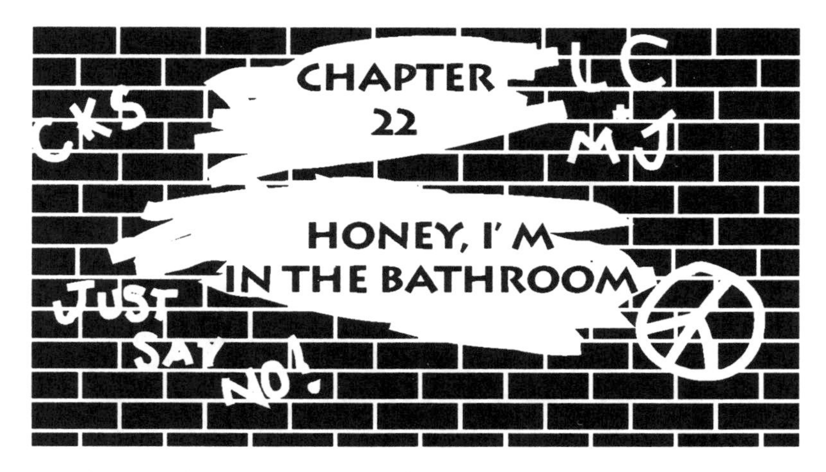

Being "occupied" in the bathroom is one of the most vulnerable places to be. Whether you're taking a bubble bath, a hot shower, or "sitting down" to read ***Dirty Fighting***, you're practically defenseless. This is just a natural fact.

The number of techniques you can employ in the bathroom while the tile floor is covered with soapy water or while you're in the middle of reading page 20 is severely limited.

The best defense while in the bathroom is several containers of easily accessible cleaning fluids (preferably caustic). This can be a spray bottle filled with ammonia, or a wide mouthed container filled with drain cleaner. Stroll the aisles of the supermarket or local hardware store to decide what's "best" for your assailant.

The method is to simply throw or splash the contents into your attacker's eyes. After that, depending upon the harshness of the chemical and your aim, nature will take its course.

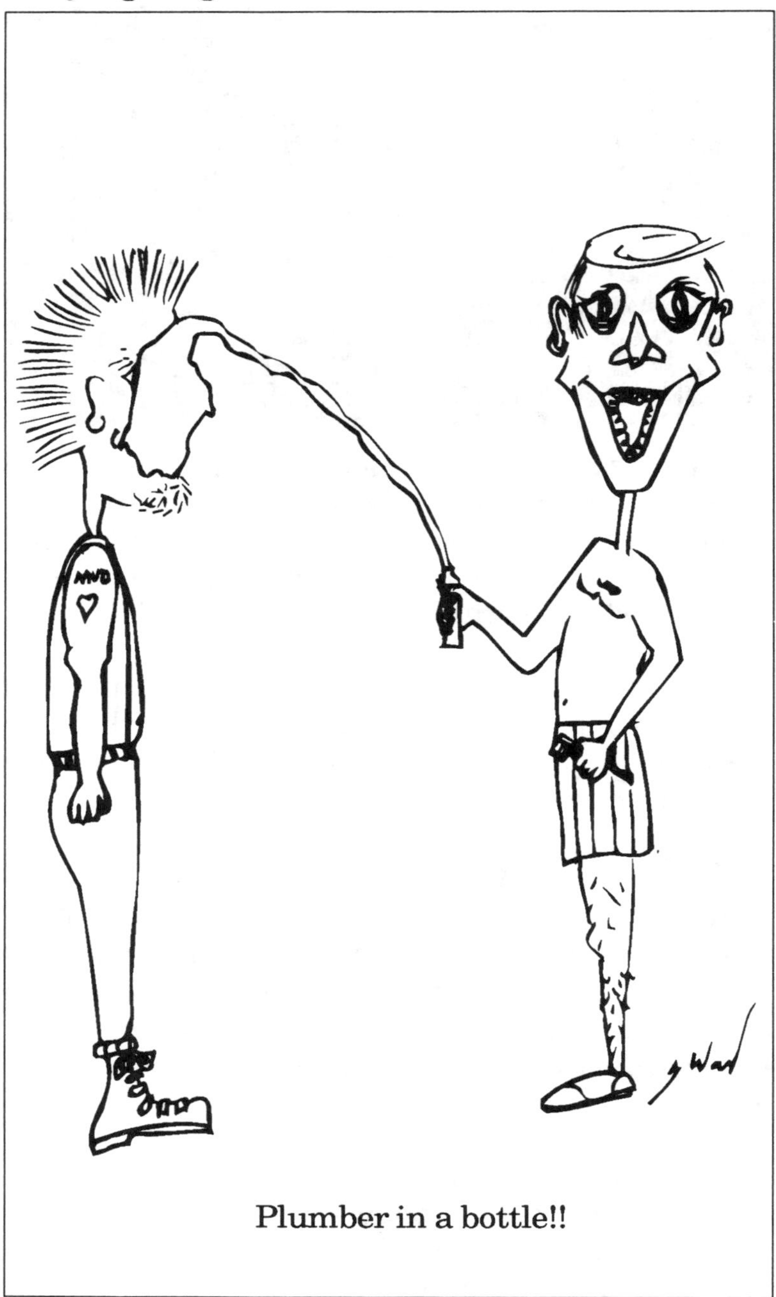

Plumber in a bottle!!

Since bathrooms are relatively small, they are not the place to start (or try and finish) a fight. You should get out of the bathroom at first opportunity.

Application: You're in the bathroom brushing your teeth, when you hear the back door slam. You call out, "Honey, is that you?" But there's no answer. You hear someone in the hall and ask again, "Is that you?" You open the bathroom door and this figure comes charging towards you. You spit the last of your toothpaste into his eyes and slam his head into the glass mirror. You grab for the ammonia bottle and pump a few squirts into his eyes. This should prevent your attacker from following you out of the bathroom as you dash to the nightstand for your Colt .45 and call the police.

Unclog Those Nasties!!

"If I only had a Weapon!" How many times have you made a plea along this line?

The key to always having a weapon available is to be able to **improvise**. Anything and everything can be a weapon.

Whether it be a folding chair, a lamp, or a nearby telephone...using immediately accessible objects as weapons or items of distraction should become second nature for the dirty fighter. This is just plain smart. Think about it. Why should you try and wrestle someone to the ground when you can simply crash a crystal ashtray across their head to achieve the same (or more effective) results?

Besides the obvious advantages of surprise and effectiveness, a tremendous amount of energy is also conserved. While your opponent is exhausting himself trying to fight fair, you haven't even started breaking a sweat with your office stapler smashing across his teeth. ("Office stapler"? Yes, fights can start anywhere!)

Eeny! Meeny! Mineey! Mo!

An excellent example of **improvisation** is a good quality metal nail file with both sides of the tip sharpened. The rough file section provides ideal gripping power while the point is strong enough to generate a substantial cut while executing both inward and outward slashes. Use it only for close quarters slashing and aim only for exposed flesh. Keep the nail file hidden in your hand until the last possible moment, then slash across the jugular vein located on either side of the neck. He will be "asleep" very soon. One nice thing about the nail file is that it is always handy and you won't be questioned for carrying it.

Do not attempt to cut through your opponent's clothing. You will only get him mad for "ruining his threads".

Another great weapon, though a little radical, is any cap containing a liner. No, the cap isn't the weapon...it's the double-edged razors that you've sewn into the liner. When confronted, simply take off your cap and swish it across your opponent's face. The razors will cut through the liner and slice up his face like a Veg-A-Matic! (This is an old New York trick.)

Carrying a cane or umbrella is another solution for always having a weapon available. But be smart about it; skipping down the sidewalk with your umbrella on a bright, sunny day without a cloud in the sky will be very suspicious and prompt too many questions to be worth it...especially if you have to use the umbrella and are asked by a wise cop why you're carrying it "on a day like today". Along the same line of thought, carrying a cane (rather than using it to walk with) as you charge up a set of stairs is another eyebrow raiser. You have to remember to play the part...always.

It is important to note that in order to use canes and umbrellas as weapons effectively, you must practice with them. It is like owning a handgun; keeping it in the nightstand drawer will not guarantee that it will protect you - you must practice with it in order to become proficient.

Application #1: You're on your way to your car after late night food shopping. You notice some strange sleaze lurking around the parking lot. Your Professional Strength Hornet Spray is conveniently packed right on top of your grocery bag. Get the picture?

Application #2: You love fishing. In fact you love fishing so much, that you tied a big five ounce lead sinker to your key chain with about eight inches of heavy cord. This handy, inconspicuous blackjack is just the thing to crack open the skull of Mr. Dirtbag.

You may want to add a key fob from a bait and tackle shop to add credibility to your story about your love for fishing. For greater control and weapon retention, tie a small loop or knot on the end of the cord so it doesn't slip through your fingers.

So you don't like fishing; then simply tie the same length of cord to your set of keys. You will gain almost the same effect as the lead sinker, providing you have enough keys (ten or more). If you haven't that many keys, add some.

The target for your lead sinker or key collection is naturally the face. The keys, especially, will create the most wonderful cutting design.

With this technique, do not swing once and observe. Swing multiple times, followed by an incapacitating kick to the knee or groin.

Application #3: It is late at night. You are waiting in the car while your husband runs into the hardware store to buy a toilet plunger. Since he exited in a rush, he left his door unlocked. All of a sudden, some punk jumps in and wants to go joy riding. He doesn't see the can of starting fluid sitting in your lap. You immediately spray it into his eyes with your left hand as you ward him off with your right.

If you plan on keeping a can of starting fluid in your car, buy a brand name (they are more reliable) and keep it accessible, not in the trunk.

If you are up to it (since it is late), you can finish him off with the ice scraper lying on the console.

Application #4: You're sitting in Dunkin' Donuts at 2:00 am enjoying a delicious Bavarian Creme donut. Two teenagers dressed in black leather jackets come in and take a seat on each side of you. They ask for your wallet. The manager is in the back of the store making a huge vat of strawberry filling, so he doesn't see what's going on. You reach for your hot black coffee and immediately splash it into one guy's face; then as you jump off the stool, you shove the handle of your coffee spoon into the eye of his friend. Make a hasty exit.

Never forget...your greatest weapon is your mind.

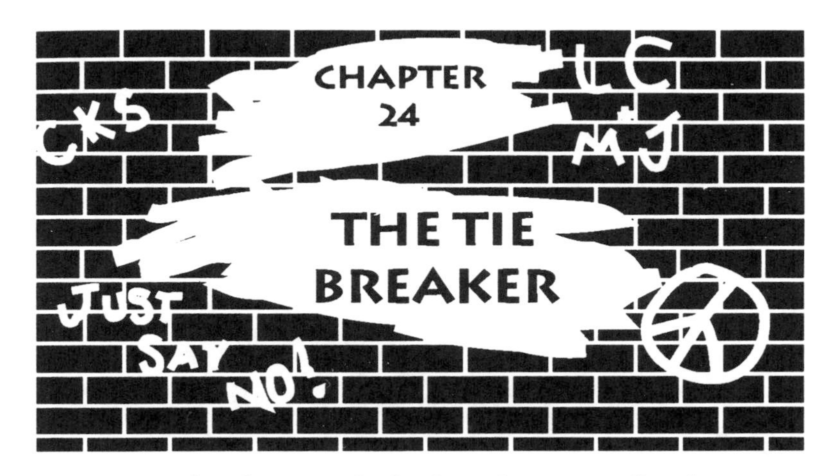

Do not be deceived, clothes do not make the man. Be forewarned that not all dudes wearing black leather jackets and high, black leather boots are out to beat you to death with chains and clubs; and not all guys wearing tie dye T-shirts with holey jeans are drug freaks looking to roll you for a few bucks. You may easily come across some hot-headed, white collar worker who wants to prove he's still as tough as he was on his 1985 high school football team. This kind of hot head can be just as dangerous as your worst-imagined mugger; for he can be just as determined; and determination, depending on its intensity, can dictate the success or failure of an attack.

As with hair pulling, gripping your opponent's tie is very effective in controlling where you want your attacker to go...whether it be into a wall or nearby telephone pole. The method is to simply grab and give a powerful, sharp, consistent pull. It is important that the pull is consistent or, if at best, increasing in force. Otherwise, your opponent will take advantage of the slack in your pull to regain his balance.

Nice Tie!!

Naturally, clip-on ties and bow ties are exempt from this technique.

Application: You're driving home from work when some yuppie in back of you is swerving in and out of traffic in his brand new BMW.

You decide to put an end to his dangerous shenanigans and box him in alongside a big, 18-wheel, tractor trailer with your 1973 Chevy Impala. As you look in your rearview mirror, you see him giving you the usual sign of "thanks". Well, your exit is coming up, so you begin getting into the right lane. As you turn off and pull into White Castle for a sack of burgers, you notice that this clown is right on your bumper. As you stop to go inside, you hear his car door slam and see him charging towards you. As he cocks his right hand back for a Ralph Kramden haymaker, you spit in his face, grab hold of his tie, and sharply pull him into and through the large pane window. As his head plows through the many shards of glass, his determination will have poured out into a large crimson pool, allowing you to continue on your merry way.

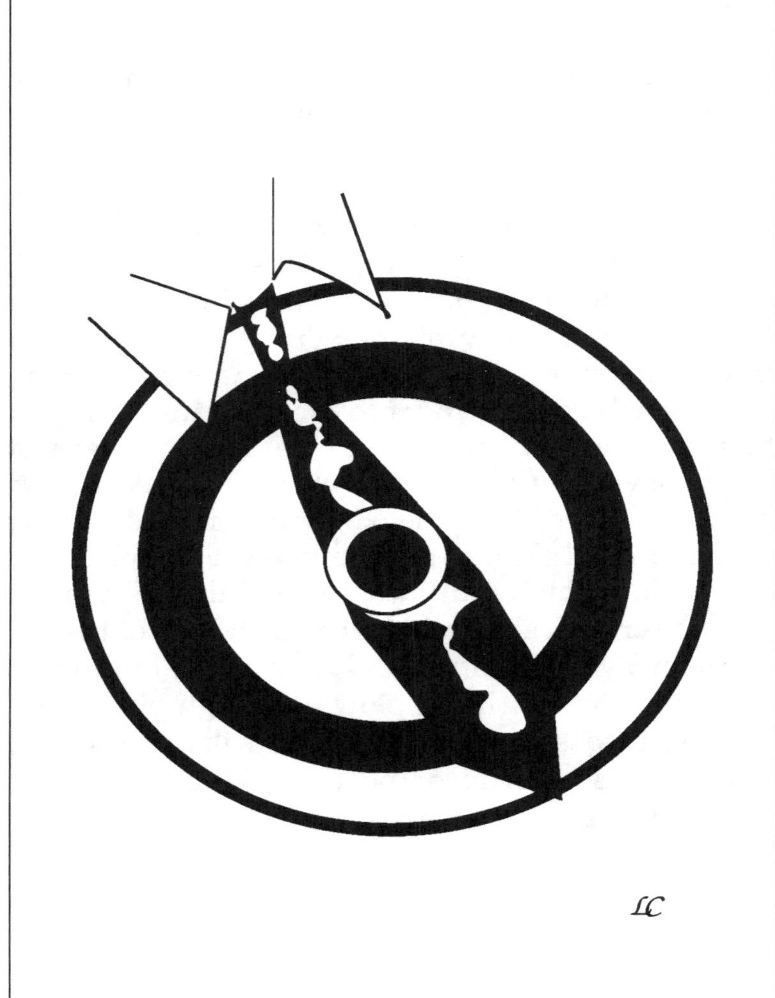

Tie-Breaking Target!!

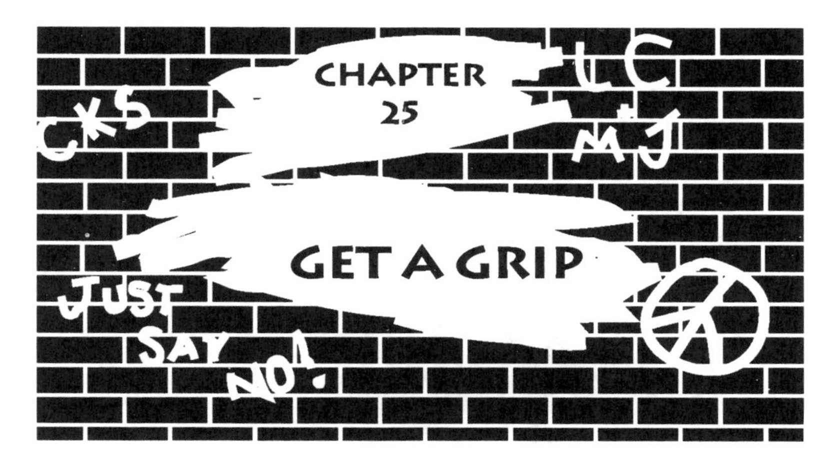

Why do school yard fights and bar room brawls always seem to be preceded by some sort of grabbing? Who knows, especially when hitting is much more effective? Anyway...

Since the odds are in your favor that whatever fight you may be in will involve some grabbing, it is important to know how to grab.

The key thing you need to remember is to always grab clothing, never bare skin...unless, of course, it is an ear or finger. It is too easy for your opponent to twist out from under an arm grab or escape from a leg hold when either you or he are covered with perspiration. Simply put, the excessive sweat reduces the friction necessary to effectively maintain a grip. In addition, the girth of your opponent's arm or leg may be substantially more than your grip can take command of and control. Clothing provides the means by which a strong grip can easily be accomplished, effected neither by perspiration or girth. Furthermore, with clothing, your grip will be more secure due to being able to completely close your fist around the material.

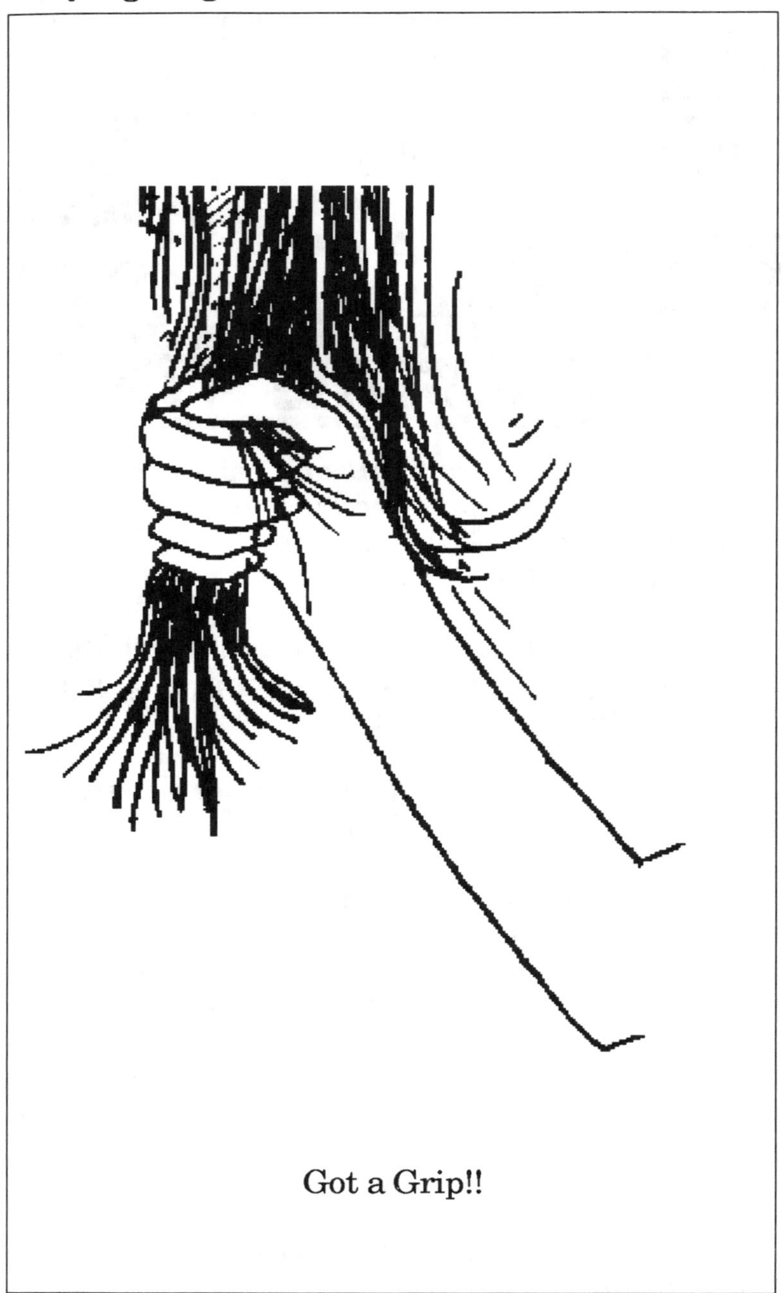

Got a Grip!!

Grabbing hold of your opponent is occasionally necessary in order to control a mild, incoming charge. Though a strike is definitely much more effective, grabbing may be (legally and morally) more warranted, such as instances where a drunk is simply harassing you for money.

Grabbing may be used to redirect an opponent's movement into another tangent (line of force) away from you. This redirection of force may be applied in a variety of different circumstances: after you've struck your opponent and they are disoriented, in response to a surprise attack from your opponent when close physical contact has suddenly been made, or in the case of the harassing drunk.

Do not use grabbing as an alternative to hitting (unless warranted); your opponent may get tired of it faster than you and be the one to throw the first punch.

In a serious confrontation, do not fall into the trap of having the act of grabbing escalate into a wrestling match on the sidewalk. If you're ever knocked to the ground and your opponent starts with the wrestling, use the ground as a weapon to bang his head against.

Suggestion: Make arrangements to sit in on a judo class or tournament to get a true taste of how effective grabbing your opponent's clothing can be. Better yet, sign up for judo instruction...it's worth just knowing how to fall correctly.

Application: You've just kicked your opponent in the groin and you're about to grab his hair and ram him into the park bench. Suddenly you notice, he's bald...he has no hair to grab! But...you remembered reading in ***Dirty Fighting*** about how effective grabbing your opponent's clothing can be, so you grab the back of his collar and smash him into the bench just as easily!

Admittedly, most of your attackers will be men. However, the day may come when you' re pitted up against some woman built better than your high school football coach...and just as masculine.

If you're a woman finding yourself confronted by such a beast, or have even been accused of stealing away your best friend's boyfriend and the smell of blood is "in the air"...biting, clawing, and hair pulling may need to be followed up by a few other dirty fighting techniques, such as:

1) Your attacker happens to be wearing a nice sweater with a lovely sweater pin. After you spit in the witch's face, grab hold of the sweater pin and stab her with it as though you were chopping up a big block of ice for your weekend party. Think "Norma Bates".

2) You're at a big company office party, when some drunken babe comes over and accuses you of dancing too close with her husband. You notice the huge brooch in her gown with the l-o-n-g stick pin. As

Check Page 108 for Results!!

you splash her with your drink (before she does it to you), grab the brooch and reinsert the pin, but not into the dress, into her.

3) This "would be" biker chick comes up to you and tries to rough you up in front of the gang in order to gain acceptance into its elite membership. After spitting her in the face, suddenly grab the pewter skull dangling from her pierced ear and yank it out. If this "would be" biker babe is wearing the latest in choker necklaces, and it's one of those made from a motorcycle chain or dog chain, grab hold of it and lead her right into the hot Harley exhaust pipe. (Just think, maybe you'll be the one they ask to join the club).

Try Pinning This One on Me!!

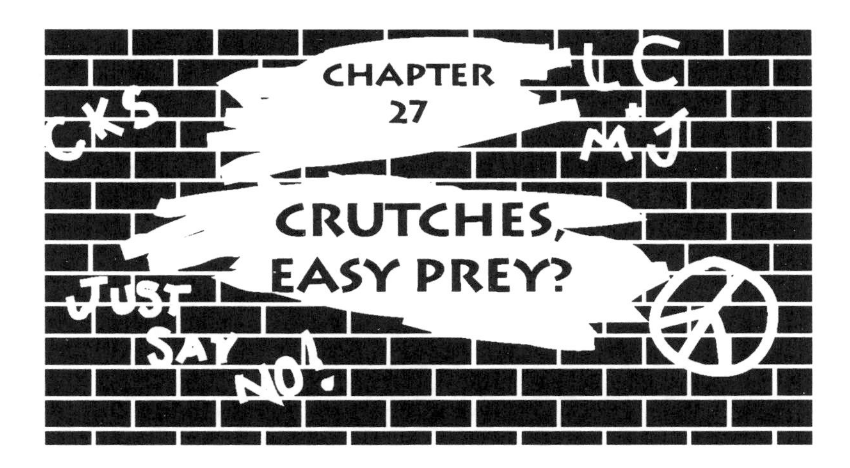

Being dependent upon crutches makes you an ideal target for the bad guys. However, crutches may be used to your advantage by simply converting them into a large, handy club.

Naturally, the more severe your injury, the more you must rely on the crutch(es) for your stability and support. Hence, your attack must be swift and brutal with no opportunity for your opponent to continue their attack. Remember, a quick getaway is out of the question.

The best method for attacking with the crutch is to simply swing the tip of it upwards into your opponent's groin. Then as his knees fold and he sinks to the ground, immediately follow-up with a crashing blow with the crutch across your opponent's skull.

You may also wish to remove the rubber tip from the crutch to further pommel or "spear" your opponent with. This is especially **dirty** when you're using metal (aluminum) crutches.

Handicapped Parking!

The upward groin swing is best practiced against a low hanging heavy bag; one in which the bottom of the bag is at about groin height. Swing the crutch straight out at first, using the armpit as your natural pivot point. Later, work on swinging out the crutch at slightly different angles. Most importantly, never swing the crutch in a large arc movement; not only will you severely jeopardize your own balance, but you may "catch" the crutch on a nearby obstacle such as a street sign, chair, or bystander.

If you happen to be knocked to the ground while on crutches (which may very well happen), use the crutches to smash your opponent's shins. Note that "shins" is plural...you have two to aim for, and both shins cannot be protected at the same time!

After your opponent drops to "your level", you can attack his eyes, his groin, bite his ear off, or further use the crutch to beat him with.

Application: You're hobbling down the street when some thug steps in front of you calling you "4 Legs" and demanding your money. As you politely refuse, he begins to step forward. Immediately spit into his face and swing the tip of the crutch into his groin. As your assailant falls forward, swing the crutch up again, but aim for his face - trying to catch one of those crutch bolts or wing nuts on his nose or eye socket. This will generate a real nasty gash.

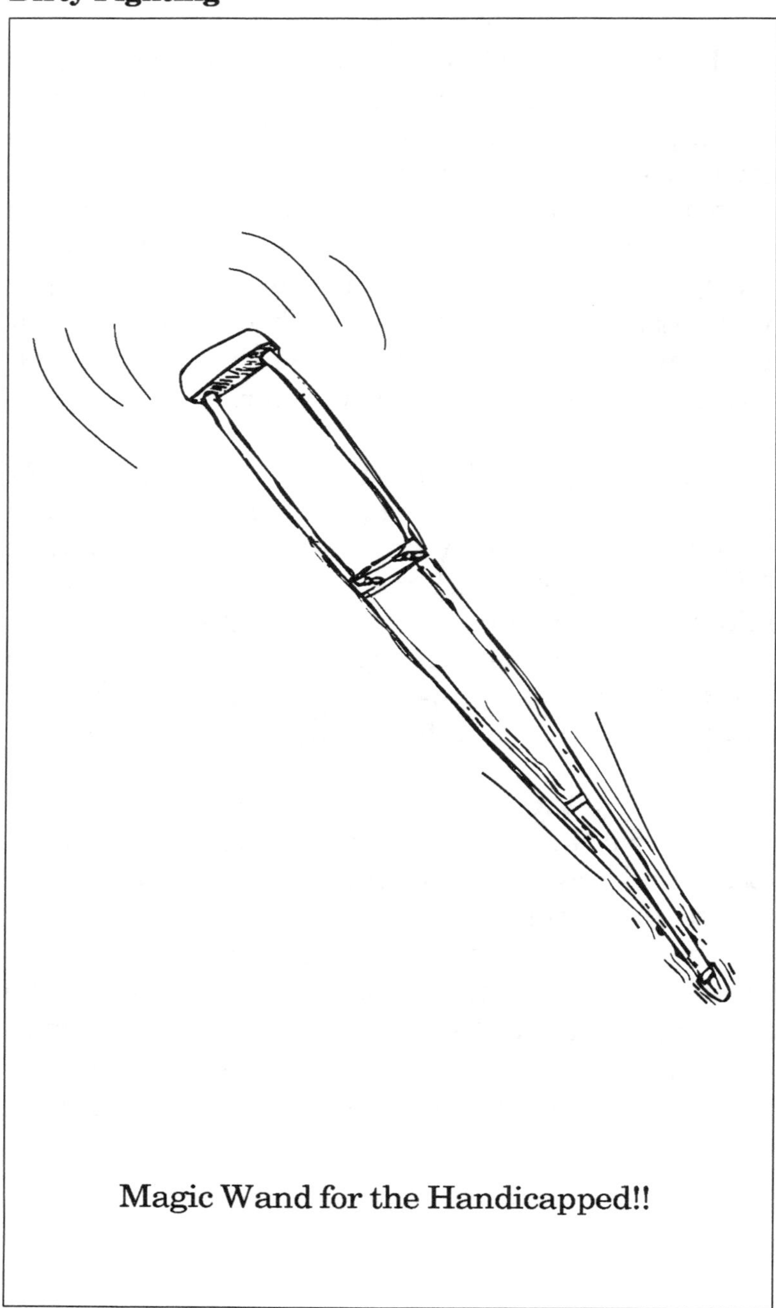

Magic Wand for the Handicapped!!

Keeping your chin up is something which should be done by your opponent, not you. Occasionally, you'll be confronted by Mr. Tough Guy who will arrogantly inflate his chest and stick his chin out. If he's about one foot or less away, thrusting the heel of your palm up and under his chin will not only snap his neck back, but will forcefully drive him away from you. As your opponent's neck snaps back and he reels backward, his hips will naturally be thrust forward, setting himself up for a perfect groin kick.

The ideal time to execute this technique is when your opponent is talking. Not only will his mind be absorbed in constructing "tough guy" sentences, but you will have a 50/50 chance to nail him while his jaw is open rather than closed. The advantage? There's a good possibility that you may shatter several of his teeth as they slam into one another. And if you're real lucky, your opponent may take a big chunk out of his tongue!

The palm heel technique is easily delivered to the underside of the chin by an up and backward move-

Keep Your Chin Up Chum!!

ment. This movement can be a follow through thrust or a quick snap; it's only important that some force be put behind it (like your own body weight). The palm heel should not be executed straight back "at" your opponent.

Hint: When delivering this technique, bring your palm up as close to your opponent's chest as possible. This path constitutes a "blind spot" for your opponent, thus giving you the advantage of surprise.

Application: You're tearing up the dance floor at your local disco while "Staying Alive" screams through the speakers. You accidentally step on some girl's foot and immediately apologize. It just so happens that her Italian Stallion boyfriend doesn't accept your apologies and wants to show how "bad" he is in front of his woman. He approaches you with the inflated "pecs" and the protruding chin and asks you to step outside. Since you don't want to miss the rest of the dance (and who knows what's waiting outside), you decide to end it right here. Immediately spit in his face and thrust the heel of your palm into his chin. As he loses his balance backward, let a swift kick fly into his groin.

You Can't be a Pussy and Win!!

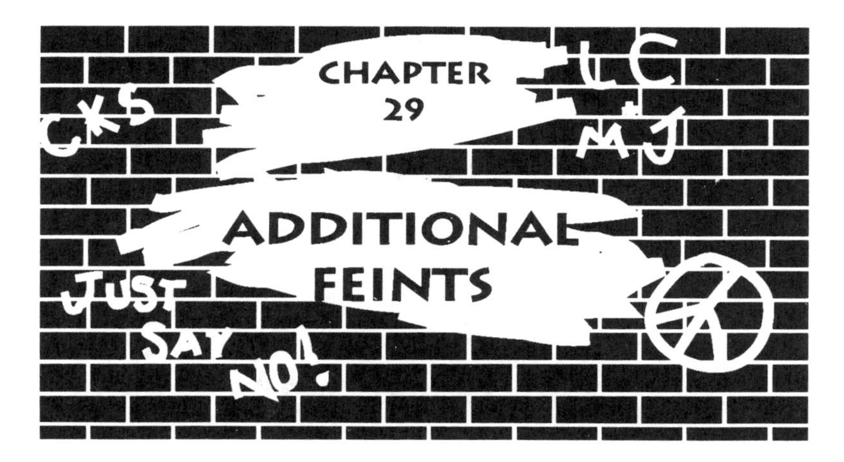

The secret to feinting is nothing more than a con game. You must convince your opponent that you are going to execute a particular technique. If your opponent does not believe your feint, that you are not going to attack, you will be the one who gets hit.

The successful feint may employ eye movement, body movement, a good rap (convincing piece of dialogue) or any combination thereof.

The highly successful feint occurs when your opponent has already experienced pain from an attack which you now use as a feint; for your opponent has learned once that this movement has caused him pain in the past and he doesn't want to relive the experience.

Here are just a few feints that you might try:

Look at your opponent's groin, look at your opponent's eyes, slightly move your leg and then attack his eyes.

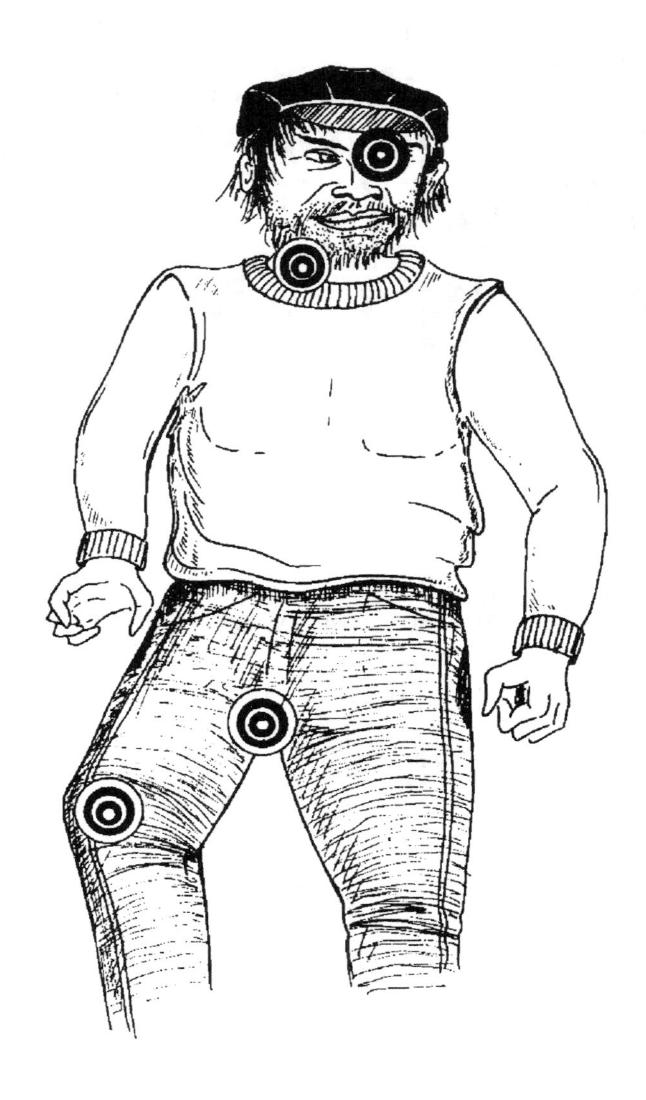

Choose His Poison!!

Assuming a stance similar to a boxer's, cock your right hand back for a real "power punch". Cock your arm back again, this time a little bit further. Your opponent is now very much aware of the windup punch you're about to deliver. Now, suddenly execute a left finger jab to the eyes.

Look over the opponent's shoulder as if there is someone behind him. The secret is to be convincing, not to try for an Oscar-winning performance. If your opponent does not fall for it the first time, try it again. You might even want to add a little head movement as though you were saying "yes" to a would-be sneak attack. If your opponent fails to turn around, check out his eyes, they often reveal what he is thinking...probably something like what he's going to do if there is someone behind him. If he seems engrossed with the idea that maybe there is someone behind him, spit in his face and execute a swift kick to the groin. This is one technique you can partially practice on friends, trying to get them to turn around or ask "who's there?" Obviously, since they're friends, both the spit and the kick are eliminated from your performance.

If your opponent is only out to rob you or simply beat you up, where sexual harassment/attack is not the motive, pulling down your pants' zipper is a real charmer (whether you're a guy or girl). Where do you think his eyes are going to be focused? As soon as his eyes have left contact with yours, spit in his face and kick him in the groin.

Along the same line...

You're standing in front of your attacker who's shooting off his mouth about how is going to smash in your face. As he's busy telling the world, generate a huge smirk across your face. Not only will he start getting more angry, but his curiosity will most likely compel him to ask "What's so funny? What are you laughing at?" You look and point at his groin and convincingly tell him "You talk tough, but you look like a little school boy standing there with your zipper wide open." Now he will either look at his fly, taking his eyes off of you, or will drop his hand(s) to check if what you're saying is true. Either way, the opening has been set for your attack. (Hint: do not try and kick your opponent in the groin with this particular feint; his attention will be too well focused in this area to guarantee a successful hit.) This technique works great if other people are standing around; for the fear of embarassment will be on your side.

Here's one I've used a lot. While walking down the street, you notice a group of questionable individuals who definitely do not look like your friendly accountants out for a noontime stroll. Unzip or unsnap your jacket as though you were carrying a gun. Do not stick your hand in as though you were auditioning for Godfather 4; just unzip it. This technique is especially effective if it is freezing cold outside; for why else would anyone unzip their jacket?!

Remember, feinting needs to be convincing.

Dirty fighting techniques must succeed the first time through. Otherwise, you may not get a second chance. The reason for this is that you have already informed your opponent of your intentions to fight dirty. And most fighters do not take to this lightly. Relaying your intentions will undoubtedly make your opponent mad, but it may also prompt him to begin fighting dirty himself, even if he had no original intentions of doing so. You must essentially "beat your opponent to the punch".

Do not attempt to gruelingly fight it out with your opponent, exchanging punches for punches, challenging force against force. Use your brains. Your opponent did not attack you with the expectation of losing. You must cheat by using every dirty trick in the book.

Always remember...punching is an art. To do it correctly, the wrist must be straight, the shoulder must be loose, the hips must rotate, the legs must spring, the center of gravity must be properly positioned, etc, etc. The perfect punch is an accumulation of finely-tuned movements accomplished in a split second, requiring the correct muscle groups to be tensed at exactly the precise moment.

Unless you plan to devote the many hours it requires to become both effective and proficient, don't bother– you'll only end up breaking your wrist against your opponent's thick skull.

Attack on the opponent's inhale. This is difficult to properly time unless your opponent is out of breath and has begun to breathe heavily. However, his strength and reaction time are practically non-existent while inhaling. Try it yourself...inhale quickly and try to perform a precise, strength-requiring feat. You'll be amazed at what you can't do.

Do not adopt the habit of holding your breath when a fight is about to ensue; simply breathe normally. The brain needs a constant supply of fresh oxygen in order for it to function both quickly and clearly.

As stated in the movie Nighthawks: "Hesitation kills". So whether you flick a boogie or spit in his eye, imediately follow-up with your attack. Do not wait for your opponent to realize what has happened or allow him time to regain his composure/anger.

After the initial attack, use follow-up techniques or run away if you feel you cannot take on your oponent alone (or if he has friends to help him). Never initiate an attack, **then** watch what happens, **then** wait for your opponent to recover, **then** attack again. Attacks should be 1, 2, 3. Not 1, pause, 2, pause, 3, pause.

Never stop the attack against your opponent until they are physically unable to utter the words, "I give up." I've seen many fights where the winner eased up on their attack as the loser pleaded for mercy - only to have their opponent retaliate more determined and vicious than before!

If you decide to grant some mercy to your opponent, be wary and on guard. Always be prepared...never surprised.

Try to employ attacks that flow together naturally...

A *good* example is the kick to the groin followed by the hair pull to the ground. In this situation, the opponent has collapsed forward at the waist, providing you with their hair in easy reach.

A *bad* example would be a groin kick followed by a punch to the throat; the opponent has collapsed forward at the waist, but has bent over in such a manner as to leave the throat unexposed for the punch.

Never place your back against a wall, unless fighting multiple assailants; then, use the wall as a stationary weapon to slam your opponent's head into. Note also, that if your back is to the wall, you've seriously reduced your chances of escaping.

Always retain your balance. The moment you lose your physical balance, you lose your mental balance as well. Without mental balance, the fight will be lost.

Think **K.I.S.S.** **K**eep **I**t **S**imple **S**tupid. The more complicated your attack, the more chances of something going wrong.

PRACTICING SUGGESTIONS

When practicing finger jabs, clawing, or other attacks to the eyes with a partner, safety goggles should always be worn.

An improvised target for practicing eye jabs can be made with a stiff piece of 2-foot square leather or heavy cardboard hanging from the ceiling. You can also use one of those foam heads that hairdressers mount wigs on, but you will have to chase after it after each blow.

Practicing should be done with someone whom you can trust, someone who can control their distance so a practice kick to the groin doesn't end up with someone squirming on the floor. Also, do not work out with someone who cannot control their temper - who may actually try and claw you in the eyes when things get hot.

Note that full body protection is not necessary when practicing the majority of dirty fighting techniques, since very few require any real strength. Speed and accuracy is what is important.

Here is a simple exercise for mastering control over your distance:

Practice extending your arm straight out in front of you towards an object with the intention of having your fingers (or fist) stop within one inch of the object. After you can accomplish this with relative ease, try extending the arm out at a different angle with the same intention of coming within one inch of the object. When your one inch distance remains consistent from any angle, begin adding speed to your movements. Later, reduce the distance to about one-halfinch and continue altering the angles. As before, when your distance remains consistent throughout, increase your speed.

The importance of controlling your distance is essential not only in knowing when to stop (pull) your punch in practice with a friend, but also how far enough you can be from your opponent and still be able to scratch his eyes out.

Finally, you may wish to graduate to a distance of one-quarter inch, aimed at an expensive family heirloom, but this well-beyond the scope of ***Dirty Fighting***.

Add variation to your practice so that your techniques are not routinely defended against by your partner. Avoid establishing a rhythm; that's often how boxers get "nailed".

Constantly train through mental conditioning. Always be busy thinking, "What would I do if someone did this?" or "What would happen if I was in this situation?". This mental conditioning will help prepare you by developing a sense of confidence while unconsciously developing your motor skills. That is why athletes perform their techniques over and over in their heads; it causes their movements to feel more natural when the time comes to actually perform them.

Conclusion: There are only a few things to remember...but first and foremost, never forget that the fight is first won in the mind. And this is not by the planning of techniques and preparation of strategies, but by attitude.

All your attacks should be executed with an animalistic attitude of uninhibited determination. Don't be nice...gentlemen never win fights.

Never stop until your opponent is no longer a threat.

Practice those techniques which you find are easy, those which you feel comfortable and confident with. Discard those which you find are awkward and cumbersome.

There are no rules...ever.

THE 1 HOUR CHINA CONTRARIAN BOOK

Four Things Everyone Is Getting Wrong About China Business

Jeffrey Towson
Jonathan Woetzel
Thijs Boevink - Editor

Ebook
ISBN-10:0-9914450-5-8
ISBN-13:978-0-9914450-5-9

Paperback
ISBN-10:0-9914450-6-6
ISBN-13:978-0-9914450-6-6

Version 2017.05.01

10 9 8 7 6 5 4 3 2 1

TABLE OF CONTENTS

III. CHINA CAN INNOVATE BIG TIME

IV. AT HOME AND ABROAD, CHINESE COMPANIES CAN BEAT YOU FAIR AND SQUARE

APPENDIX. OTHER CHINA STUFF TO KEEP AN EYE ON

ABOUT ONE HOUR CHINA

"Without question, the best 60 minutes you will spend on China."

—Jonathan Anderson,
Emerging Markets Advisors

"One hour with this book will make you an expert on business in China."

—Dick Gephardt,
Majority-Minority Leader, U.S. House of Representatives, 1989-2002

"This book simplifies China in a very elegant and smart way. These distinguished authors tell you clearly what you most need to know right now."

—James McGregor,
author of *One Billion Customers: Lessons from the Front Lines of Doing Business in China*

"The One Hour China Book offers an even-handed and well-illustrated insight into the seemingly chaotic and often self-contradictory China prospects in a pleasantly easy read."

—Rui-Gang Li,
Chairman of China Media Capital

"For most people, the intellectual return on time spent reading this book is almost unrivaled."

—Value Walk

ALSO BY THE AUTHORS

The One Hour China Book (2017 Edition): Two Peking University Professors Explain All of China Business in Five Short Stories, by Jeffrey Towson and Jonathan Woetzel (2017).

The One Hour China Consumer Book: Five Short Stories That Explain the Brutal Fight for One Billion Consumers, by Jeffrey Towson and Jonathan Woetzel (2015).

No Ordinary Disruption: The Four Global Forces Breaking All the Trends, by Jonathan Woetzel, Richard Dobbs, James Manyika (2016)

What Would Ben Graham Do Now?: A New Value Investing Playbook for a Global Age, by Jeffrey Towson (May 21, 2011)

Capitalist China: Strategies for a Revolutionized Economy, by Jonathan R. Woetzel (August 13, 2003)

Operation China: From Strategy to Execution, by Jimmy Hexter and Jonathan Woetzel (December 18, 2007)

INTRODUCTION

China is big. It's also complicated.

That's our standard attention-grabbing (and controversy-generating) opener. That China is really big and complicated. It's important to be provocative in publishing.

This is our third "speed-read" One Hour China book and it is different than the previous two. The original One Hour China Book and One Hour China Consumer Book provided frameworks for China business and Chinese consumers. They provided models on which you can hang the various China facts, news and events.

This book, instead, is a collection of our articles and essays from the past two years. And this essay collection approach follows from our super-provocative opening statement. As China continues to grow and develop, it is exploding in complexity. In response, we have gone more granular - and have focused more and more on small, niche situations and questions. As China gets bigger and more complicated, you have to go small, hence an essay collection.

And we tend to focus on situations where we think the conventional wisdom is wrong. Hence, this One Hour China Contrarian Book. We hope you find it helpful.

WHO WE ARE

Between us we have over 40 years on the ground in China. We have somehow become "old hands" at China business, which is a bit disconcerting (as is getting older in general). We both write books and articles – and Peking University in Beijing is our academic home. But our primary careers are in management consulting (Jonathan) and private equity / advisory (Jeff). Note: since the last book, Jonathan has also become one of the three co-directors of the McKinsey Global Institute (MGI) so you will see a lot of MGI research cited in his sections.

Jonathan Woetzel

We are both really thinkers by profession – and we have both ended up living with one foot in China and the other out. Jonathan lives with his family in Shanghai and Los Angeles. Jeff lives between Beijing and New York, but is kind of a global nomad (and perpetual conference speaker).

Jeffrey Towson

This China-to-the-world position has given us front row seats to one of the history's most important events: the rise of China and its collision with the rest of the world. To be able to spend our careers studying this event has just been tremendous good fortune. We'd like to claim it was good strategy, but it was probably just luck.

FOUR THINGS EVERYONE IS GETTING WRONG ABOUT CHINA

This book is a collection of essays and articles that really make four contrarian points. These points are:

- China needs smarter, not faster growth.
- Yes, Chinese consumers are rising but they are changing even faster. And they are disrupting almost everything.
- China can innovate big time.
- At home and abroad, Chinese companies can beat you fair and square.

We'll explain each in the subsequent chapters. We hope they are helpful to you.

Thanks for reading and cheers,

Jonathan and Jeff
June 2017

An important clarification. These essays are by each of us individually. This means Jonathan and therefore McKinsey & Co have absolutely nothing to do with any article, essay or point by Jeff.

Finally, a special thanks to Thijs Boevink for doing the editing for this book. Thijs was one of our top students at Peking University in 2016. He is a cum laude graduate of the Rotterdam School of Management with an MSc in finance. He is someone you should absolutely have on your radar.

POINT I
CHINA NEEDS SMARTER NOT FASTER GROWTH

The fall in China's nominal GDP growth from 10% to 5% has been a huge story for the past several years. And every year, there is a lot of media commentary when China's latest GDP growth numbers get released. For example, there was a ton of discussion when growth recently fell from 7.6% to 6.8%. And while this is entertaining, it is mostly nonsense.

First, keep in mind, nobody knows what the real GDP for China is, let alone the GDP growth over 12 months. Measuring the economic output of a country of 1.4B people is difficult – and it is impossible without a huge amount of uncertainty. So these reported growth numbers are directional at best (i.e., it's slower than last year). And they are certainly not accurate to a tenth or even a single percentage point.

Second, slowing growth is just fine. What matters is whether it is smart, productive, and good growth or whether it is bubbly, over-leveraged, and fake growth. It also really depends on where you are looking. Car sales in China are at about 5% growth now but SUV sales are growing at over 10%. Growth in e-commerce, online gaming and healthcare is currently phenomenal. But economy beer is growing at only around 3% now. And so on. So it really depends where you are looking.

Finally and per our opening statement, China is now just really big and really complicated. Trying to boil all this down to one surprisingly specific number is becoming ridiculous. If you are looking at growth in China, you need to look for real growth. You need to look for smart growth. And you need to go industry by industry, and probably even smaller than that.

In this section, we discuss this at length in five short essays about China's changing GDP growth, productivity and debt.

CHINA NEEDS SMARTER NOT FASTER GROWTH

By Jonathan Woetzel

China's economy is slowing from its blistering pace of recent years. Premier Li Keqiang told global leaders attending the World Economic Forum in Davos that this slowdown is no cause for concern, that there would be no hard landing, and that China is now focused on ensuring an "appropriate" pace of economic expansion.

His remarks point to an important truth about China's growth in the years ahead. It is not the precise rate of growth that is the key issue, but what drives that growth. What's important for China is changing its growth model from one that is investment-driven to one that is productivity-led.

AN AGING CHINA

China, in common with many other countries, is aging. Over the past 50 years, rapid population growth meant expanding labor pools, boosting growth. But population growth is now slowing—with major implications for growth.

China's labor force could shrink by one-fifth over the next 50 years. On current trends, China could have one dependent aged 65 or more for every two working-age citizens. Peak employment could occur as early as 2024, concludes a McKinsey Global Institute (MGI) report *Global growth: Can productivity save the day in an aging world?*

PRODUCTIVITY IMPERATIVE

This puts the onus even more heavily on raising productivity to drive GDP growth. China has already made huge strides to improve productivity, which has increased 14-fold over the past 50 years, and been responsible for three-quarters of China's growth over that period.

But because of dramatic demographic change, even at those rapid rates of productivity growth, over the next 50 years China could grow at a 30 percent slower rate—an average of 5.3 percent a year compared with 7.6 percent over the past half century.

That would still be a significantly faster rate than in other major economies but there is plenty of scope for China to accelerate its productivity-growth rate and do even better.

THE OPPORTUNITY

About 80 percent of the productivity opportunity MGI has identified in emerging economies such as China comes from catching up with best practice in operations and business approaches; the rest can come from innovation, not just in the use of technologies but through imaginative ways of managing businesses and processes.

Let's look at four key sectors:

1. Today, China's huge automotive industry has 67 percent of the productivity of the average in developed economies. But if China were to move from its large number of small plants to a smaller number of large operations, productivity could rise by up to 50 percent

2. In agriculture, there is huge scope to boost productivity. Nearly 30 percent of the labor force is employed in agriculture and labor productivity in Chinese agriculture—$4,200 per worker—is only 5 percent of the US level. A number of factors explain this, the most important being the predominance of subscale farms in China. The average farm plot is 0.5 hectares compared with 10 hectares in the United States. In addition, mechanization is low at 60 percent compared with 70 percent in South Korea and 96 percent in the United States. Taking Zhejiang Province as an example, the evidence suggests that mechanization could reduce the labor needed to cultivate rice by more than 40 percent. This of course has an implication for migration which is one reason why government policy in this area has been cautious

3. China is transforming retail through e-commerce players like Alibaba. Labor productivity in China's online retail sector has been two-thirds of the US level, a much narrower gap than the 75 to 80 percent gap in retailing overall. If China's online retailers were to match the productivity of their counterparts in other countries, this could boost overall retail productivity by 14 percent. In physical retailing, moving to modern formats is the most powerful way to boost productivity. Here, too, China is making progress. The share of traditional grocery stores fell from 31 percent of grocery sales in 2000 to 15 percent in 2009, largely through regulation encouraging more consolidation in the sector.

4. The productivity imperative is particularly acute in health care because spending is growing so fast. China's spending has almost tripled in five years and is projected to reach $1 trillion by 2020. Making health care more efficient is a potent source of productivity. Today, patients spend an average of 10 days in hospital, which is expensive. But there are ways to reduce hospital stays. Japan has cut the (still lengthy) time people spend in hospital by nearly a week since 2000. It did so by moving toward less invasive surgical procedures, and using digital technology to monitor patients at home.

Slower growth can be smarter growth and China can continue its march toward prosperity. Productivity and innovation need to be front and center of this journey.

CHINA IS GROWING JUST FINE FOR AN ADVANCED ECONOMY

By Jonathan Woetzel

For three decades, the inexorable rise of China has been a fundamental force in the global economy. Questions about what China will do next have long shaped economic analysis and corporate strategy. What sub-segment of manufacturing will it tackle next? Where will it invest? How will its rising wealth and soaring new cities affect world markets?

Today, China has risen. It has passed Japan in GDP and is closing in on the United States. This raises new questions about China's role in the global economy. It should also encourage new ways of thinking about China and the world.

Even now, the focus of China watching has shifted from concerns about how it might dominate a new world order to whether its slowing growth is a problem. Whether Chinese GDP grows by 7 percent per year or by 6 percent or less, it still adds a Canada to global GDP every 2 years.

More importantly, we should be concerned about how China deals with the forces behind its slowing growth. Some of these forces, such as aging and skill gaps, are seen around the developed world. Some, such as rising labor rates, are standard for developing economies that are moving up toward middle-income status. Others, like the soaring debt that has attended China's rapid urbanization, are unique to China.

THE CHALLENGE OF AN AGING CHINA

Aging, for example, will have outsized impact on China. As the world's most populous economy, China will be hit hard by the costs of aging. The number of Chinese 55 or older is expected to rise to over 33 percent by 2030. Public pension expenditures are expected to rise to 10 percent of GDP by 2050, and public health costs are expected to rise even faster. By 2040, China could have more dementia patients than in all advanced economies combined. All this happens at a relatively low level of per capita income.

Indeed, China is getting old before it will get rich. Usually dependency ratios (the number of minor children and senior citizens in proportion to the number of working age citizens) drop in developing economies as they industrialize and only rise when they have become middle-income or wealthy. China's dependency ratio has already begun to climb and could approach current EU levels (above 30 percent) by 2020.

Aging also challenges China's labor-intensive growth model. In the past few decades, tens of millions of Chinese workers entered the global labor force, helping to drive GDP growth and lifting hundreds of millions of Chinese out of poverty. This demographic dividend is disappearing because of aging and a low birth rate. In January 2013, China's National Bureau of Statistics announced that the country's working- age population actually fell in 2012 and it has continued to decline since.

At the same time, China faces a looming skills gap as its economy moves to a more consumption-based and services-oriented economy, a pattern that all developed economies have followed. Despite a dramatic expansion of post-secondary education, China could have 23 million too few high-skill workers (loosely defined as those with college degrees) by 2020.

DEBT, INFRASTRUCTURE, AND FINANCIAL STRAIN

China also has a difficult path to navigate between maintaining healthy growth and controlling the enormous debt that has been incurred to support that growth, particularly in the years since the global financial crisis.

About a third of this debt is associated with booming real estate markets, including debt of supplier industries such as construction, steel, and cement. These industries now have excess capacity and real estate demand has softened. Also, it is not clear how the shadow banking system that has also funded these industries can cope with defaults—even though it seems to be widely assumed that the government would intervene to avoid a debt crisis.

The most troubling debt challenge, however, may be in local government finances. With the encouragement of the central government, local governments have run up over $2.9 trillion in debt since 2009, much of it issued by off balance-sheet entities known as local government financing vehicles. The central government has initiated reforms and efforts to restructure local government debt—including by allowing provinces to roll loans into bonds, but demand for these bonds has been weak.

At the same time, urbanization continues apace with 100 million more citizens coming into cities between 2014 and 2020. Continuing urbanization is important for continuing growth, but will require additional investment in housing and infrastructure—and additional financing.

ADVANCED CHALLENGES FOR AN ADVANCING ECONOMY

If we think about all these challenges, we begin to see China in a very different light. The qualities and strategies that have brought it so quickly to the forefront of global economies will continue to serve China, but are not sufficient to tackle these challenges.

Modern China finds itself confronting a full range of economic and social challenges that are characteristic of advanced economies, even as it remains a developing economy (at least by the metric of GDP per capita).

CHINA SHOULD BOOST PRODUCTIVITY, NOT REPRODUCTIVITY

By Jonathan Woetzel

China's one-child policy, finally ended by Beijing and replaced with a two-child stipulation, caused untold heartache for tens of millions. Worldwide, an estimated 1.5 million girls are not born each year because of sex-selective abortion in four countries alone (Azerbaijan, China, India, and Vietnam). Many young Chinese men have been left with no prospect of ever finding a wife.

But it is economics, not social equity, which forged the policy and has now ended it. Deng Xiaoping, who imposed the policy in the late 1970s, did so to ensure that the "fruits of economic growth are not devoured by population growth". Now China's leadership is reacting to the rapid aging of China and its threat to growth.

Partly as a result of its one-child policy, China experienced a sharp decline in the fertility rate from about 5.8 births per woman in 1960 to 1.6 in 2012. Its working-age population peaked in 2010, and MGI analysis suggests that the labor force could shrink by one-fifth over the next 50 years. There could be one dependent aged 65 or over for every two working-age citizens. Peak employment could occur as early as 2024.

But the truth is that China, like many other countries, is past the point where policy can influence demographics. Although the partial relaxation of the one child policy in China's urban areas has led to a small increase in fertility, and there is bound to be something of a spike in births as a result of the latest policy change, the economic impact in the short term will be limited.

In any case, declining fertility and shrinking labor pools appear to be globally irreversible. Consider that birth rates in China's East Asian neighbors—where there are no policy restrictions—are also very low. Even higher incomes doesn't appear to be persuading women to have more children. In Japan—which has invented a new word *shoshika*, which means a society without children—the fertility rate has only been above the "replacement" rate in eight of the past 50 years.

At the margin, governments could offer incentives for women to have more children including, for instance, fully funded, high-quality child-care services, and tax breaks for parents with children. In Europe, Denmark, France, Finland, France, Sweden, and the United Kingdom all have high levels of public spending on child care as a percentage of GDP, and they have among the highest fertility rates in the region. But such policies are costly and take a long time to have an effect.

In reality, the only option for China to mitigate the impact on growth of a rapidly aging population is productivity—not reproductivity. And productivity has to include women. China's full productivity potential will not be realized without fully using the economic potential of women.

MGI's research on gender equality finds that if Chinese women were to participate equally in labor markets (including hours worked and sector participation) as men, as much as $4.2 trillion, or 20 percent, could be added to China's annual GDP in 2025. Even in a more conservative scenario in which China matched the progress toward gender equality of its fastest-improving neighbor, $2.5 trillion or 12 percent could be added to China's GDP in that year.

Productivity has increased 14-fold over the past 50 years. But even if it maintained impressive historical rates of productivity growth, demographic headwinds mean China's economy would grow at a 30 percent lower rate at an average of 5.3 percent a year over the next 50 years - compared with 7.6 percent over the past half century.

The good news is there is considerable scope to accelerate productivity growth in China. Take the auto sector, which has about 67 percent of the average productivity in developed economies; consolidation of the industry into a smaller number of large car plants could boost productivity by up to 50 percent. Labor productivity in Chinese agriculture—$4,200 per worker—is only 5 percent of the US level.

A number of factors explain this, the most important being the predominance of subscale farms in China. The average farm plot is 0.5 hectares compared with 10 hectares in the United States. In addition, mechanization is low at 60 percent compared with 70 percent in South Korea and 96 percent in the United States.The productivity of China's burgeoning online retail sector is only two-thirds that of the United States.

Simply adopting and spreading best practice in the way companies—and governments—conduct their operations would capture three-quarters of China's productivity potential. The rest would come from technological, operational, and business innovations that push the frontier of China's growth potential.

The ending of China's social experiment in birth control is welcome social and humanitarian relief. But China's aging economy will need the power of gender parity and the power of productivity to sustain itself in the years ahead.

CHINA'S DEBT IS NOT THE BIG PROBLEM (YET)

By Jonathan Woetzel

China's total debt quadrupled between 2007 and 2014, which was about one-third of the $57 trillion in debt added globally during that period. Can this possibly be safe?

The key question is whether China can slow the growth of its debt without unduly crimping GDP growth, which already has fallen to the lowest rate in nearly a quarter century.

My conclusion is that China's debt situation warrants careful monitoring. In broad terms, China's debt has moved from a developing economy level (158 percent of GDP in 2007) to advanced-economy status (282 percent in 2014, a bit higher than the United States and Germany). Not only does the speed of this debt buildup raise alarms, so does its composition. Almost half of new debt is flowing into the property sector and related industries, and around 30 percent of debt is provided by a shadow banking industry, whose lending standards and exposures are not easily discerned.

That's not ideal but it may be manageable. Household and government debt are both low, even by the standards of developing economies, while debt of non-financial corporations is high. China has the financial wherewithal to weather a debt-induced crisis. And China's government is taking steps to reduce the risk of crisis.

There are three areas of potential risk: a concentration of debt in the property sector; reliance on shadow banking; and the large debts of local governments.

- **Real estate.** Nearly half the debt jump in China from 2007 to 2014 went to real estate development or related industries such as steel and cement. While Chinese households are not, in general, over-extended with mortgage debt, a deep and prolonged housing slump could have a huge impact on the construction sector, which accounts for 15 percent of GDP and includes tens of thousands of small players who would not be able to meet their debt obligations. The steel and cement industries, which already have excess capacity, would also suffer.

- **Shadow banking.** The so-called shadow banking system—consisting of unregulated non-bank lenders—accounted for 30 percent of all new credit between 2007 and 2014. Shadow banks, such as trust companies, raised money from wealthy investors seeking high returns and lent to players in real estate as well as to companies that cannot qualify for bank loans. Not only is shadow banking concentrated in real estate, the quality of its underwriting is not known—nor is the total exposure of shadow banks. One trust company missed its payment to investors because a single borrower—a steel company—missed a payment.

- **Local governments.** As a result of China's rapid urbanization and limitations on how local governments can raise revenue, the debt of local government in China had grown to almost $3 trillion by 2014-2015. Most of this was owed by local government financing vehicles, off-balance sheet entities that are used to fund investments in infrastructure, social housing, and other types of construction. The ability of some local governments to pay back their debts is in question: a 2014 audit found that more than 20 percent of recent loans were used to pay older debts and that almost 40 percent of debt servicing and repayments were funded by land sales.

Chinese policy makers are certainly aware of the risks associated with unsustainable debt and are taking steps to reduce them. The government has imposed punitive interest rates for mortgages on second homes, and banned purchases of third homes to cool off the real estate market.

In shadow banking, the government has imposed stricter product marketing rules on trust companies. To reduce reliance on land sales and LGFVs, the government has allowed cities to issue municipal bonds (on a limited basis).

The state also has changed the incentives for local governments, emphasizing sustainable economic development, social harmony, and environmental protection, which takes pressure off cities to build more costly infrastructure. If these measures are sufficient—and are implemented consistently—China's debt might remain merely a potential concern for the global economy.

5 REASONS WHY CHINA'S ECONOMY WON'T COLLAPSE

By Jonathan Woetzel

A widely held Western view of China is that its stunning economic success contains the seeds of imminent collapse. This is a kind of anchoring bias, which colors academic and think-tank views of the country, as well as stories in the media.

In this analysis, China appears to have an economy unlike others—the normal rules of development haven't been followed, and behavior is irrational at best, criminal at worst.

There's no question, of course, that China's recent slowdown is both real and important for the global economy. But news events like China's stock-market plunge and the yuan's changing value versus the dollar reinforce the refrain, among a chorus of China watchers, that the country's long flirtation with disaster has finally ended, as predicted, in tears.

Meanwhile, Chinese officials, worried about political blowback, are said to ignore advice from outside experts on heading off further turmoil and they are said to be paranoid about criticism.

My experience working and living in China for the past three decades suggests that this one-dimensional view is far from reality. Doubts about China's future regularly ebb and flow. In what follows, I challenge five common assumptions.

1. CHINA HAS BEEN FAKING IT.

A key tenet of the China-meltdown thesis is that the country has simply not established a basis for a sustainable economy. It is said to lack a competitive, dynamic private-enterprise structure and to have captured most of the value possible from cheap labor and heavy foreign investment already.

Clearly, China lacks some elements of a modern market economy—for example, the legal system falls short of the support for property rights in advanced countries. Nonetheless, as China-economy scholar Nicholas Lardy has pointed out, the private sector is vibrant and tracing an upward trend line. The share of state-owned enterprises in industrial output continues to drop steadily, from 78% in 1978 to 23% in 2014. Private industry far outstrips the value added in the state sector, and lending to private players is growing rapidly.

In fact, much of China's development model mirrors that of other industrializing and urbanizing economies in Asia and elsewhere. The high savings rate, initial investments in heavy industries and manufacturing, and efforts to guide and stabilize a rapidly industrializing and urbanizing economy, for example, resemble the policies that Japan, South Korea, and Taiwan followed at a similar stage of their development. This investment-led model can lead to its own problems, as Japan's experience over the past 20 years indicates. Still, a willingness to intervene pragmatically in the market doesn't imply backwardness or economic management that is heedless of its impact on neighboring economies and global partners.

Furthermore, China's recent reform initiatives are direct responses to the structural changes in the economy. The new policies aim to spur higher-value exports, to target vibrant emerging markets, to open many sectors for private investors, and to promote consumption-led growth rooted in rising middle-class incomes.

Today, consumption continues to go up faster than GDP, and investors have recently piled into sectors from water treatment to e-commerce. These reforms are continuing at the same time China is stepping up its anticorruption drive, and the government hasn't resorted to massive investment spending (as it did in 2008). That shows just how important the reforms are.

2. CHINA'S ECONOMY LACKS THE CAPACITY TO INNOVATE.

Think tanks, academics, and journalists alike maintain that China has, at best, a weak capacity to innovate—the lifeblood of a modern economy. They usually argue as well that the educational system stomps out creativity.

My work with multinationals keen on partnering with innovative Chinese companies suggests that there's no shortage of local players with a strong creative streak. A recent McKinsey Global Institute (MGI) study describes areas where innovation is flourishing here. Process innovations are propelling competitive advantage and growth for many manufacturers. Innovation is at the heart of the success of companies in sectors adapting to fast-changing consumer needs, so digital leaders like Alibaba (e-commerce) and Xiaomi (smartphones) have emerged as global contenders.

Heavy investment in R&D—China ranks number two globally in overall spending—and over a million science and engineering graduates a year are helping to establish important beachheads in science- and engineering-based innovation.

3. CHINA'S ENVIRONMENTAL DEGRADATION IS AT THE POINT OF NO RETURN.

To believe this, you need to think that the Chinese are content with a dirty environment and lack the financial muscle to clean things up. O.K., they got things wrong in the first place, but so did most countries moving from an agrarian to an industrial economy.

China is spending heavily on abatement efforts, as well. The nation's Airborne Pollution Prevention and Control Action Plan, mandating reductions in coal use and emissions, has earmarked an estimated $277 billion to target regions with the heaviest pollution. That's just one of several policy efforts to limit coal's dominance in the economy and to encourage cleaner energy supplies. My interactions with leaders of Chinese cities have shown me that many of them incorporate strict environmental targets into their economic master plans.

4. UNPRODUCTIVE INVESTMENT AND RISING DEBT FUELS CHINA'S RAPID GROWTH.

To believe this, you would have to think, as many skeptics do, that the Chinese economy is fundamentally driven by overbuilding—too many roads, bridges, and buildings. In fact, as one economist has noted, this is a misperception created by the fact that the country is just very big. An eye-popping statistic is illustrative: in 2013, China consumed 25 times more cement than the U.S. economy did, on average, from 1985 to 2010. But adjusted for per-capita consumption and global construction patterns, China's use is pretty much in line with that of South Korea and Taiwan during their economic booms.

China's rising debt, of course, continues to raise alarms. In fact, rather than deleveraging since the onset of the financial crisis, China has seen its total debt double as a share of GDP, a recent MGI study found. Much of the debt is directly or indirectly related to real estate. Local governments too have borrowed heavily in their rush to finance major infrastructure projects.

While the borrowing does border on recklessness, China's government has plenty of financial capacity to weather a crisis. According to MGI research, state debt hovers at only 55% of GDP, substantially lower than it is in much of the West. A recent analysis of China's financial sector shows that even in the worst case—if credit write-offs reached unprecedented levels—only a fairly narrow segment of Chinese financial institutions would endure severe damage. And while growth would surely slow, in all likelihood the overall economy wouldn't seize up.

Finally, the stock-market slide is less significant than the recent global hysteria suggests. The government holds 60% of the market cap of Chinese companies. Moreover, the stock market represents only a small portion of their capital funding. And remember, it went up by 150% before coming down by 40.

Rumors drive most of the volatility on China's stock exchange, often in anticipation of trading by state entities. An issue is that the direct impact on the real economy will most likely be some reduction in consumer demand from people who have lost money trading in shares.

5. SOCIAL INEQUITIES AND DISENFRANCHISED PEOPLE THREATEN STABILITY.

On this one, I agree with the bears, but it's not just China that must worry about the problem. While economic growth has benefited the vast majority of the population, the gap between the countryside and the cities is increasing as urban wealth accelerates. There's also a widening breach within urban areas—the rich are growing richer.

Urban inequality and a lack of access to education and healthcare are not problems unique to China. People here and in the West may find fruitful opportunities to exchange ideas because the pattern across Western economies is similar. Leaders of the central government have suggested policies to improve income distribution and to create a fair and sustainable social-security system, though implementation remains a matter for localities and varies greatly among them.

In short, China's growth is slower, but weighing the evidence I have seen, the sky isn't falling. Adjustment and reform are the hallmarks of a stable and responsive economy—particularly in volatile times.

POINT II

YES, CHINESE CONSUMERS ARE RISING BUT THEY ARE CHANGING EVEN FASTER. AND THEY ARE DISRUPTING ALMOST EVERYTHING

Much of the current China hope and hype is centered on increasing consumer spending – as a way to rebalance the economy, to drive regional growth and to create new growth opportunities for companies (and investors) everywhere. Virtually everyone is watching and hoping for increasing consumption by middle class Chinese these days.

The good news is this has mostly been happening. Rising Chinese consumers are now a real economic phenomenon, which definitely wasn't the case 10 years ago. Between 2010 and 2015, they increased in annual consumer spending by $1.1 trillion. That is a big number and represented over 25% of all global growth in consumption. Note: increasing consumption by American consumers was also about 25% of global growth in consumption.

Chinese consumers are now spending and this is going to increase dramatically going forward. We are really just at the beginning. For example, by 2025 there will be over 250M middle class Chinese families. As most spending happens at the household level, this is really the group to watch.

However, Chinese consumer spending is also exploding in complexity. You now have millions of sophisticated Chinese travelers spending their vacations in Paris and New York. You have rapidly rising inland consumers who are still mostly bargain hunting. You have over 300M Chinese moms, who are just a fascinating demographic. You have Chinese millennials who are spending dramatically differently than previous generations. And so on.

Chinese consumers and consumption are just getting more and more complicated. They are changing very quickly in their behavior. And these changes are increasingly rippling out into markets around the world. So yes, Chinese consumers are rising. But they are changing even faster and this is increasingly disrupting markets in China and around the world. Welcome to the new normal.

In this section, we discuss changing Chinese consumers and their growing impact on the world.

CHINA'S INCREASINGLY EMOTIONAL CONSUMERS ARE SHAKING THE WORLD

By Jeffrey Towson

Chinese consumers continue to grow relentlessly in number and wealth. This is a well-studied economic trend. But what people are missing is how the changing behavior of these consumers is now regularly shaking the world.

Suddenly when Chinese consumers start eating more meat, it impacts agriculture in the American midwest. When they discover northern Thailand as a fun destination, they flood the area with tourists. When Chinese consumers change their minds about something, it now ripples outward into the global economy. And these types of phenomena are going to become a lot more noticeable in the coming years.

The economic trend underlying this is the steady advance of China's urban middle class families. This is the group to watch. According to McKinsey & Co., Chinese urban household disposable income will reach $8,000 a year by 2020. This will be about the same level as South Korea, but in a much, much larger population. After Middle Eastern oil, Chinese urban middle class families are arguably the most valuable natural resource on the planet.

But within this big trend, an important shift is now occurring. Urban families are rapidly transitioning from "value hunters" to more emotional, aspirational and free-spending consumers.

Price-focused consumers have dominated the China story thus far. They typically have had little brand loyalty and tend to shop around for the best deals, mostly for life's necessities. Chinese companies such as Haier Group and China Vanke have done very well selling these consumers air conditioners and apartments at affordable prices.

The more emotional group now emerging, called "new mainstream" consumers by McKinsey, already has life's basics. And they have enough disposable income to buy discretionary items such as lattes and trips to Thailand.

What this new group cares about is quality, brand and how products make them feel. So they want real iPhones, not cheap alternatives, and they are able and willing to pay for them. What is fascinating about this group is that they behave fairly similarly to consumers in developed markets.

And here's the factoid that really matters. These "new mainstream" consumers accounted for about 5% of China in 2010, with value seekers then accounting for the overwhelming majority. But according to McKinsey, the new mainstream will represent over half of urban middle class families by 2020. This is the important transition that is happening right now. It is a transition from functional to emotional. From basic living to self-realization.

It means Chinese consumers are rapidly becoming much more emotional and unpredictable. Suddenly, when Chinese consumers like a movie, such as Furious 7, they can become the largest source of revenue for it.

In 2015, several multinational fast-food chains got a painful lesson in this phenomenon after media reports of alleged contaminated food in their Chinese outlets. Their global financial results took significant hits. While reported as a food scandal, this incident was really about urban Chinese families caring more about food safety now than in the past.

OVERWHELMED

Conversely, if Chinese consumers decide that a particular brand is safe or better than its rivals, companies can suddenly be overwhelmed with orders. This recently happened to Swisse Wellness Group, one of Australia's leading vitamin and supplement companies.

During the first half of 2015, Swisse, which had virtually no operations in China, suddenly found its sales into China growing very rapidly. It turned out that Chinese consumers had begun ranking its products highly on Tmall. Revenues for the year (ended in June) jumped to A$313 million ($235 million) from A$125 million a year earlier. And unsurprisingly, a Chinese company (Biostime International Holdings) quickly bought Swisse in A$1.39 billion deal.

Another example is the story of the Bobbie Bear, a bright purple teddy bear stuffed with lavender and sold by a farm in Tasmania. This small lavender farm, a retirement project of owner Robert Ravens, became inundated with orders after Chinese model / actress Zhang Xinyu posted a photo of her Bobbie Bear online. Orders surged to more than 45,000 and the farm was forced to suspend online sales, as it could not handle the demand from China.

Chinese tourists began showing up in Tasmania in droves to make purchases at the farm's gift shop. The company had to place limits on how many bears could be bought by visitors at the gift shop. Annual visitors to the farm jumped to 60,000. At one point, a hacker, presumed to have been Chinese, broke into the farm's computer system to try to place bear orders.

The point is that increasingly emotional Chinese consumers (i.e., less pure value seeking) are now regularly causing such events around the world.

INCREASING MECHANISMS

A second factor is that the mechanisms through which Chinese consumers can impact companies around the world are increasing. The Swisse vitamin example was possible because cross-border e-commerce, known as "*haitao*" in China, now lets consumers there buy overseas goods online and get them delivered to China.

Another mechanism is real estate. Every six to 12 months, Chinese consumers seem to discover a new favorite place and start buying huge numbers of homes there. This phenomenon started in Hong Kong a few years ago. Buying then switched to Vancouver and Toronto. In the last year, we have seen heavy Chinese purchasing of homes in New York and California.

Tourism is another mechanism. The number of trips abroad by Chinese tourists now exceeds 130 million a year and their travel tastes can be unpredictable as well. For example, following the 2012 hit movie "Lost in Thailand," Chinese tourists started flooding into Chiang Mai, the main tourist hub in the area where the movie was filmed. Arrivals to the city were reportedly up 500% in 2013 alone.

So two important factors are now coming together: the increasingly emotional behavior of Chinese consumers (who are growing in wealth) and a multiplication of the mechanisms by which their behavior can impact the world, often in real-time.

What this means for markets and businesses around the globe is that they can now be directly impacted by what is discussed at dinner tables, in offices and online in China. My recommendation is to start paying attention to those conversations.

(article reposted from Nikkei Asian Review, original located here)

CHINESE MOMS ARE PROBABLY THE WORLD'S MOST IMPORTANT CONSUMERS

By Jeffrey Towson

The big China consumer stories of the past year have included a vaccine scandal, food contamination scares, surging overseas home buying, and continued rising consumption by urban families.

These stories, in reality, are mostly about Chinese women as an ascending consumer class. More specifically, they are about Chinese moms, who are quickly becoming the most important consumers on the planet.

My argument for this is five points:

POINT 1: CHINESE MOTHERS ARE THE MAJOR DRIVING FORCE BEHIND INCREASING CHINESE HOUSEHOLD CONSUMPTION.

There are about 300M moms in China, making them roughly the same size as the entire US population. And they are the trifecta of Chinese consumer spending.

- First, Chinese mothers have their own personal spending power and typically contribute 50% of the family income.

- Second, they direct much of household spending. In a 2010 MasterCard report, 75% of Chinese women said they control the family spending. This can be doing most of the weekly shopping or approving expenditures above a certain level. And in some cases, Chinese wives will control the bank accounts and then just give the husband cash to use.

- Third, Chinese mothers often control the spending related to the retired parents. This is particularly true for the larger expenditures such as housing and medical costs.

So in many families, Chinese moms are effectively directing the spending across three generations.

POINT 2: CHINESE MOTHERS ARE DEEPLY FOCUSED ON THE HEALTH AND SAFETY OF THEIR (USUALLY) ONE CHILD.

Family spending control by mothers is not unusual globally. But in China it is amplified by the effect of the (now-revoked) one-child policy, the prevalence of "little emperors" and the greater health and safety concerns of living in China. Chinese moms are more concerned with the health and safety of their one child - from the water they drink, to their food, to their education, and to their general physical safety.

One interesting result of this is the different advertising for women seen in China today. In the West, we often see ads for women speaking to independence or fun. However, in China we see more focus on happy and healthy families. For example, in 2013, McDonalds China launched a "Moms' Trust" campaign which not only highlighted healthy children but also focused on long-lasting relationships. This is a contrast to fast food commercials in the U.S. which typically express fun and good food.

On the McDonald's China website, you can even find sections such as "Mom's standards, our standards" and "We care for how healthy our chicks grow".

POINT 3: CHINESE MOTHERS ARE RISING AS CONSUMERS IN THEIR OWN RIGHT.

Chinese mothers (and women generally) are important consumers in their own right. As mentioned, they typically contribute 50% the family income. And by most measures, they are more financially ambitious than women in virtually any other country. Go into any office building in Shanghai and you will see a sea of cubicles filled with white-collar Chinese women, most of whom also have a child at home.

The personal wealth of Chinese women is increasing due to

advancing careers and the delaying of marriage and children. For example, the number of high school students in China going to college is expected to reach about 40% by 2020 (up from 20-30% in 2010). But going to college and then getting a good job usually means delaying marriage, family and other commitments. In the past ten years, the average age at which women have children in China has increased from 24 to 27. And it will soon be closer to 30, which is similar to most developed countries.

One consequence of this delaying of life events is greater wealth. By the time women do marry and have children in China, they have more money and higher incomes. So Chinese moms are going to have more money to spend even before they become the primary financial decision-makers of the household.

POINT 4: MANY OF THE BIGGEST CHINA CONSUMER STORIES ARE ACTUALLY STORIES ABOUT CHINESE MOMS.

Health and wellness has become a major consumer issue in China. It shows up in almost every study. But this is really mostly a women and mom's issue. (Note: 68% of Chinese men still smoke and this number is actually rising. In contrast, only about 3% of Chinese women smoke and this number is falling.)

Consider the popular 2015 pollution documentary *Under the Dome*. This film by CCTV producer Chai Jing took air pollution to a new level of national priority. But *Under the Dome* actually offered no new information on pollution in China. What it did do was re-frame pollution as the story of a mother worrying about pollution's impact on her daughter's health. It spoke to Chinese moms.

Another example. Jiang Yilei (a postgraduate student and Internet sensation who goes by Papi Jiang) signed a 22M RMB advertising deal with a beauty products e-commerce site. Jiang has risen from obscurity to national fame in just six months with homemade videos were she plays various characters. But arguably the most popular one is of a young career woman dealing with the pressure to marry and have a baby.

Another example. In 2016, an elite school private school in Changzhou was found to have been built on polluted land. Over 500 students became ill and there were investigations and protests. But if you look at the photos of the protesters in the press, you'll note virtually the entire crowd was Chinese moms.

You can find such consumer stories all the time. From food scandals, to pollution to education to travel to family spending. It's almost always mostly about Chinese moms.

POINT 5: GET READY. BECAUSE CHINESE MOMS ARE GOING GLOBAL.

In 2015, there was a surge in Chinese women going to the California to give birth. And Chinese births in the U.S have likely reached +60,000 per year. This phenomenon even showed up in the 2013 Chinese movie "Finding Mr. Right", where a Chinese woman went to Seattle on a tourist visa to go shopping and have an American baby.

"Birth tourism" is a good example of Chinese moms starting to go global. In this case, it is about giving their child US citizenship but also about increasing their educational opportunities. Note: US citizenship not only enables sending a child to the US for school (anything from kindergarten to PhD), it also helps in getting into elite international schools back in China. The most famous recent story about "birth tourism" was that of the Chinese woman who gave birth on a plane heading to California - and she kept asking "are we in US airspace yet?".

Another example is that fertility clinics in Los Angeles have been reporting surging numbers of Chinese women arriving for services. Clinics I have spoken to mentioned 20-40% of their patients are now visiting Chinese.

A final example is the aesthetics market. Chinese women are increasingly getting on planes to get botox, plastic surgery and other treatments abroad. Again, this is different than in the West where such treatments are overwhelming done by women over 40. These Chinese women are mostly 25-40 and include lots of young moms. We are currently seeing this business boom in Thailand and South Korea – and increasingly in Hong Kong.

* * *

The take-away from all of this is that **Chinese moms are at the forefront of the rising wealth of Chinese households**. They are the front of this incredibly important wave. And given the increasing concerns about GDP growth and economic re-balancing towards consumer spending, I argue that makes them the most important consumers on the planet right now.

(reprinted from Nikkei Asian Review, located here)

YOUNG CHINESE CONSUMERS ARE REALLY IMPORTANT – BUT ARE REALLY DIFFERENT

By Jeffrey Towson

There are approximately 200M Chinese between 15 and 24 years of age. They are about 15% of the population and have, by and large, been raised in relative abundance.

Unlike previous generations, these young Chinese mostly have no memory of hunger or extreme hardship. The urban ones have mostly grown up in modern apartments with modern conveniences. They are a very different and pretty interesting group. For example:

1. **They are more brand loyal than other Chinese middle class consumers.** They are also more interested in trying new products.

2. **They are more emotional and less concerned with being frugal.** If you are focused on up-trading consumers, this is your group.

3. **They are really confident about their own financial futures.** This group is super-confident, which enables spending.

Basically, this is the demographic the whole world has been waiting for: **emotional, confident, big-spending Chinese consumers.** They are also a demographic that is more similar to consumers in developed economies.

Young Chinese consumers have a more Western approach to shopping

% of Consumer Respondents by Segment

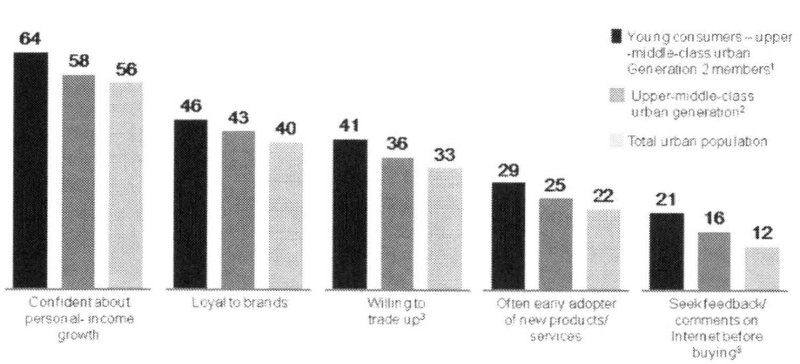

1 People born after the mid-1980s and raised in a period of relative abundance
2 Annual household income of 106,000–229,000 renminbi (equivalent to $16,000 to $34,000 in 2010 real terms)
3 Personal-care-product example

Source: 2012 McKinsey survey of 10,000 Chinese consumers

Finally, it almost goes without saying that young Chinese consumers are a lot more wired. They are overwhelmingly online and 90% have mobile phones. If you want to reach young Chinese consumers, you will need a strategy for smartphones and the Internet.

CHINA'S 220M SENIORS AREN'T SPENDING AND AREN'T GOING TO

By Jeffrey Towson

There are lots of articles about the rapid aging of China – and about seniors as a massive consumer demographic. And this is basically true.

- According to the National Bureau of Statistics, in 2015 China had 222M people above 60 years old, about 16% of the population..

- This demographic is expected to increase to 25% of the population by 2030. This will put Chinese seniors at the same percentage as most developed countries - and would mean **an increase to 345M seniors**.

- China will soon be the most aged of the BRIC countries and will have the largest elderly population on the planet.

That is the trend everyone is talking about as a possible market opportunity. However, the problem is this big consumer demographic just isn't spending much money. The demographic is there but the market is not. And the main reason why is shown in the below graphic.

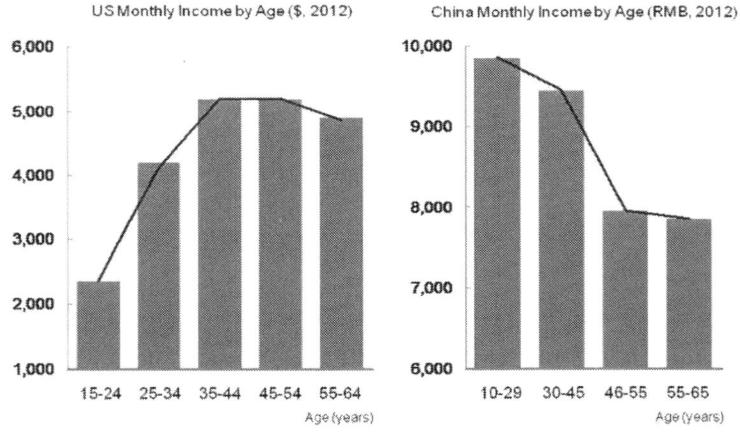

There is a huge drop-off in income for Chinese over age 45. In the chart, compare China on the right with the US on the left. It is almost an inverse of income by age. And we would see the same picture if we compared to virtually any other G20 country. Older Chinese consumers are not wealthy.

There are a couple of reasons for this:

- Most people in China now over age 55-60 had many working years during the Cultural Revolution (1966-1976). This gave them colorful stories but little wealth and few marketable skills.

- Afterwards, many wound up in State enterprises, many of which were then shut down. SOEs were also not a big opportunity for wealth creation.

These experiences also ingrained in the Chinese elderly a visceral frugality, not unlike the generation of Americans who lived through the Great Depression. Not only do they have low incomes but they are very frugal.

The take-away is that if your business is selling something to Chinese seniors, don't get caught up in the big demographic numbers. This population doesn't have a lot of money and generally won't spend it anyways. Dreams of selling millions of nutrition drinks and senior housing units in China have, by and large, not come true.

That said, this is a historical anomaly and will disappear over time. And as this happens, the incomes of Chinese seniors should grow faster than other groups.

WHAT CHINA SLOW DOWN? MCDONALDS, ADIDAS, AND OTHERS ARE ACCELERATING.

By Jeffrey Towson

Is China's growth really slowing? It depends on where you're looking.

Certainly, some China industries are slowing, such as smartphones, construction materials and basic automotive. But others, such as entertainment and the Internet, are growing really fast.

I keep an eye out for companies that are actually accelerating, relative to their past performance. What companies are gunning the engine this year? Below are 8 companies that were accelerating in China in 2016.

1. ADIDAS AG

The German sportswear company has about 9,000 China stores. And they booked China revenue of $2.5 billion in 2015, up 18% from the previous year.

Yet in March 2016, Adidas announced plans to open 3,000 more China stores within the next five years. They also plan to double the number of China cities in which they operate.

That's a pretty impressive acceleration for an already big number. Adidas China head Colin Currie described their China business as "healthy and sustainable" (pretty understated I think) and he cited continued "sports participation growth" as part of the reason for their expansion.

2. MCDONALDS

In May 2016, McDonalds announced plans to have 3,500 China restaurants by 2020. That's a big increase from their already big +2,200 stores. However, even at 3,500 outlets, China will still be only 6% of their stores globally. And they will still be behind KFC in China. So there is a lot more runway for them.

Note: it took McDonalds about 20 years to reach 1,000 stores in China (achieved around 2010). But they then doubled to 2,220 stores in just a few years. So the planned increase to 3,500 is really a continuation of this current acceleration. And all of this is part of a larger planned expansion into Asia, where they have plans to open 1,500 stores total by 2020.

3. STARBUCKS

In 2016, CEO Schulz said Starbucks will open 500 stores a year in China for the next five years. That will take Starbucks from about 2,000 to 4,500 China outlets. That number sounds big. But it's actually not for China.

Starbucks is unique on this acceleration list in that they are the only one without a major China competitor. There is no local China giant flooding local money into opening coffee outlets. That is tremendous good luck. They should put the pedal to the floor and grab as many markets as they can while this unusual situation lasts.

4. ZARA

Spanish Zara (i.e., Inditex) has about 514 stores in China. And they opened 60 of these in 2015. This makes China about 7% of their stores globally (+6,900 stores), but over 25% of their new store openings annually.

Assuming Zara follows the same growth plan going-forward, this will mean +60 new stores annually, which is well over 10% growth.

5. H&M

Zara's competitor H&M has an even better China story. In fact, fast fashion in China generally seems pretty fantastic. In 2015, H&M opened 86 China stores, out of 413 new stores globally. So like Zara, China is over 20% of their global growth annually (in stores, not sales).

Assuming a similar plan going forward, we can probably expect another 80-90 stores and +20% China growth annually. It's pretty impressive.

6. APPLE'S RETAIL STORES

Back in January 2015, Apple announced plans to increase from 15 to 40 China stores within two years. They hit 33 stores in January 2016 and 40 stores in July 2016. So even with slowing smartphone sales in China, Apple is continuing to expand their retail footprint fairly significantly.

7. AMOREPACIFIC

AmorePacific is a competitor of L'oreal but is not as well known in the West. They are South Korea's largest cosmetics manufacturer and they have been growing dramatically in China. They opened over 300 China stores in 2015 alone. That was up about 15%, given their now +2,500 stores in China. I expect similar growth going forward.

AND FINALLY, TACO BELL HAS COME BACK AFTER 13 YEARS

Yum! Brands has recently re-opened Taco Bell in China. This is about 10 years after they closed their last China outlet on their first attempt. Ok. This isn't an acceleration story but I really like Taco Bell and have waiting for them to come back for a long time. So they made my list. Now if we can just get Krispy Kreme to come back and give China another try?

CHINESE CONSUMERS ARE NOW EATING WAY TOO MUCH

By Jonathan Woetzel

The rising wave of obesity around the world and its health and economic costs cannot be ignored. Walking down the street you literally can't miss it. This is also no longer a "western" problem. Today, 62 percent of the world's obese people are in developing countries.

Some facts on this:

- More than 2.1 billion people—nearly 30 percent of the global population—are overweight or obese today.
- That's nearly two and a half times the number of adults and children who are undernourished.
- Obesity is responsible for about 5 percent of deaths worldwide.

- The global economic impact from obesity is roughly $2.0 trillion, or 2.8 percent of global GDP, roughly equivalent to the global impact from smoking or armed violence, war, and terrorism.

A PROBLEM FOR CHINA?

China's rapid industrialization and urbanization is boosting incomes. Higher incomes, generally, mean more food and often a more sedentary lifestyle. The risk of obesity rises with income.

In China, the prevalence of obesity in cities is now three to four times the rate in rural areas. This is a reflection of higher incomes in urban areas and therefore higher levels of nutrition and food consumption - and often less active labor. The prevalence of obese and overweight people rose at 1.2 percent a year in Chinese adult males between 1985 and 2004 and 1 percent a year in adult females. Today, the top social cost for China is air pollution, the second is smoking, and obesity ranks ninth. But that ranking could rise very quickly.

There is also worrying evidence that obesity can entrench itself more quickly in countries that have experienced food scarcity in the recent past. Take the Micronesian island of Nauru, which, until the mid-20th century, experienced repeated food shortages and starvation. Once food poverty was a thing of the past, the prevalence of obesity and type 2 diabetes soared to among the highest worldwide. In 2010, 94 percent of men and 93 percent of women were overweight, and approximately 71 percent of the population was obese.[2]

WHAT COULD BE DONE?

Without action, almost half of adults in the world will be overweight or obese by 2030. MGI has conducted economic analysis of obesity that looked at 74 interventions that are being discussed or piloted somewhere in the world (including restrictions on advertising of high-calorie food and drink, calorie and nutritional labeling, and public-health campaigns).There was sufficient data for 44 of these interventions. The conclusion was that each single intervention is likely to have only a small impact on its own. Only a systemic, sustained portfolio of anti-obesity initiatives will work—implemented on a large scale.

Everyone needs to play their part from government to retailers, consumer-goods companies, restaurants, employers, media organizations, educators, health-care providers, and individuals.

Individual responsibility for health and fitness is vital, but experience shows it is insufficient on its own. People need help and that means changes to the environment in which they are making choices. Such changes include changing marketing practices, and restructuring cities to make it easier for people to exercise. It will be well worth China experimenting with solutions and trying them out—before obesity takes hold and becomes a more expensive problem.

[1] Barry M. Popkin, "Will China's nutrition transition overwhelm its health care system and slow economic growth?" *Health Affairs*, volume 27, number 4, 2008.

[2] *Nauru country health information profile 2011*, statistical annex, World Health Organization.

AFFORDABLE HOUSING IS A GROWING PROBLEM

By Jonathan Woetzel

The affordable housing problem, like everything in China, is bigger than in most other places. But China could also show the world how to close the gap faster and better than ever before.

CHINA IS RUNNING TO KEEP UP WITH HOUSING DEMAND

Because of rapid urbanization, demand for housing has outstripped supply in China. And this is despite a building boom that has created a massive construction sector that now accounts for about 15 percent of GDP. China's cities may not have the sprawling squatter communities that are often seen in the large cities of other developing economies, but it has tens of millions of housing units that either do not meet basic standards for cost, essential amenities (plumbing, electricity), or space (even using a localized standard of 50 square meters for a four-member household compared with 90 square meters in the United States).

Across China, 60 percent of households in cities of more than 7 million people cannot afford basic housing at market rates. In total, China's affordable housing gap (the difference between market-rate housing costs and 30 percent of income for households in lower-income groups) equates to about $180 billion per year, or about 2 percent of GDP. That's about 28 percent of the global gap of $650 billion, based on data for 2,400 cities.[1]

Not surprisingly, the housing affordability gap is concentrated in China's largest cities, where residential property prices rose by as much as 86 percent from 2010 to 2016. Today, about 14 million low-income households in China are financially overstretched by rent or mortgage payments exceeding 30 percent of income. And, based on current trends in urbanization and income growth, the number of low-income households in Chinese cities could rise by 56 million by 2025. Shanghai could add 2.3 million low-income households and Beijing could add 2.5 million. Four of the five cities in the world with the fastest-growing populations of low-income residents are likely to be in China.

---

1 In MGI's recent research, *A blueprint for addressing the global affordable housing challenge*, we looked at the affordable housing gap (i.e., the number of households that live in substandard dwellings and/or pay a disproportionate share of income for housing) in cities around the world. We estimated that 200 million urban households in Asia, Africa, and Latin America live in substandard housing; and 62 million of those are in China.

FOUR WAYS TO CLOSE THE GAP

Can China halt the expansion of the affordable housing gap and begin to move millions of urban households into decent housing that they can afford?

In our research, we find that there are four opportunities globally to improve the supply of affordable housing: securing land for development at the right price and in the right place for low-income households to integrate into the economy; improving productivity of construction firms; raising the efficiency of building operations; and expanding access to housing finance. China is making progress in most of these areas and its model may be scalable to other emerging markets.

1. USE THE LAND YOU'VE GOT

To start with, to reduce land hoarding and speculation in cities, China imposes penalties on owners who leave tracts undeveloped. The government also releases public land for development every year, granting 70-year land leases. And local governments are starting to pursue innovative approaches to incentivize private developers to include affordable housing in their projects. In Nanjing a pilot land auction was held last December in which developers competed to maximize affordable housing once a target price was reached. Hong Kong provides a model for successful transit-oriented development that includes affordable housing.

However, there are still shortcomings in China's land policies. District and city governments often do not coordinate to integrate transport and land planning. Industry continues to squeeze out other uses for land. Limits on building heights reduce the opportunity for densification. And while government's own programs for building affordable housing are significant—from 2012 through 2015, government built an estimated 20 million units—local implementation of the new policy varies. In some places, for example, the migrant workers who are most in need are still excluded from publicly-financed housing. And rehabilitating low income areas – so-called villages in the city - requires a clear understanding of how housing fits into an overall plan to integrate low-income Chinese into the modern economy and begin to raise their incomes.

2. GET CONSTRUCTION PRODUCTIVITY UP

Around the world, we find that advanced design and construction methods, including use of industrial approaches (such as greater use of pre-fabricated components), can cut construction costs by as much as 30 percent, helping make new construction more affordable. Singapore excels in construction management with its CONQUAS construction quality assessment system. Chinese companies, such as the Broad Group, have pioneered new low-cost construction processes. But overall China's construction industry faces the same productivity challenges that are seen around the world, including rising wage rates. Average monthly wages in Chinese construction rose by 76 percent from 2008 to 2012.

3. MANAGE BUILDINGS PROFESSIONALLY TO CAPTURE SAVINGS

While China spends about half as much as EU-27 nations on operation and maintenance as a share of housing costs, it has taken steps to improve efficiency. From 2006 to 2011, China funded energy-efficient retrofits (new heating systems, insulated windows, etc.) for 182 million square meters of housing in northern provinces. And in 2004, China regulated the property management industry and introduced a certification scheme for provider firms to encourage professionalism and cost-effective service.

4. PROMOTE LOW INCOME HOUSING DEVELOPER FINANCE

Financing affordable housing could also be an opportunity for China's banking industry. We estimate that it would take $300 billion to $400 billion a year in mortgage underwriting to close the affordable housing gap globally and perhaps a fourth of that would be needed in China. Today China's housing market is still very underleveraged making it difficult for low income households to get access to housing especially in tier one cities.

* * *

China is building housing at a breathtaking rate. But not enough of that is getting to meet the needs of its most vulnerable urban residents. Affordable housing can be an economic opportunity for China. We estimate that $94 billion to $104 billion per year would need to be spent on construction to close China's affordable housing gap by 2025. Even a small share of that could help to engineer a soft landing for the construction industry as the building boom slows. By adopting market mechanisms and continuing to innovate, China can capture this opportunity, make affordable housing a reality for all and show the world how to close the gap at scale.

CHINA'S CONSUMERS WILL CONTINUE TO SURPRISE THE WORLD

By Jonathan Woetzel and Jeffrey Towson

China has an awesome consumer story. Yet lately you can't pick up a newspaper, go online, or watch television without hearing continual moaning about the country's slowing economic growth and the need for "rebalancing."

The reality is that Chinese consumers are going to continue to increase in wealth and complexity. And if you're worried the country's economic importance is declining, you're probably looking at its performance the wrong way.

DON'T WORRY ABOUT CONSUMER SPENDING AS A PERCENTAGE OF GDP

As in most developing Asian economies, China's early growth was based on savings, investment, and exports. You get your population to save, move to the cities, work in factories, and make stuff. This is sold, and cash is brought back home for investment. Plus, you get some foreign investment as well.

This process enabled China to develop its infrastructure largely with its own cash. That, by the way, is not the norm. Developing economies typically borrow from foreigners and then default. For example, American states such as Mississippi and Florida were chronic defaulters on foreign debt as they initially developed.

One of the downsides of this investment-first approach is that it makes consumption look small and often like it's shrinking. Chinese consumption decreased from approximately 51 percent of gross domestic product in 1985 to 43 percent in 1995. And to 38 percent in 2005, and to 34 percent in 2013. By comparison, consumption is around 61 percent in Japan and about 68 percent in the United States.

China's small and decreasing consumption percentage is one reason why people keep talking about "rebalancing"—the need for the economy to become driven more by consumer spending than investment and exports. But here's the problem

First, from 2000 to 2010, the size of the Chinese economy more than doubled. So consumption grew from around $650 billion to almost $1.4 trillion. Regardless of its relative percentage of GDP,

China's consumption has been growing faster than just about any other country's in absolute terms.

Second, just getting consumer spending back to 43 percent of GDP, the level in 1995, would have a huge impact on "rebalancing." It would also create the largest consumer market in the world.

Third, most of these numbers are wildly inaccurate. Consumer spending is nearly impossible to measure in such a big, complicated economy. Combining a vague number with two other big vague numbers (investment and net exports) is fuzzy math. Until economists start putting uncertainty estimates on their China calculations, relative percentages aren't worth paying too much attention to.

HOUSEHOLD INCOME IS WHAT MATTERS, AND IT'S GREAT

One number you really want to keep in mind is household income. You can't have consumption without income. And here's where it gets really awesome. China's household income is huge. It is now likely above $5 trillion a year.

Plus, lots of income is unreported, so this is really the lower boundary for true household income. Developing economies—especially the BRIC nations of Brazil, Russia, India, and China—are frequently grouped together, but Chinese consumers now dwarf all the others in terms of household income.

RISING DISCRETIONARY SPENDING IS THE EXCITING PART

Discretionary spending is buying stuff you like but don't need. Or you only sort of need. And, fortunately, people seem to have an endless appetite for non-essentials such as entertainment, skiing, cafe lattes and so on.

Chinese citizens are now moving beyond being able to only afford the basics of life, and their discretionary spending is taking off. Growth in spending on annual discretionary categories in China is forecast to exceed 7 percent between 2010 and 2020, and growth of 6 to 7 percent annually is expected in a second category of "seminecessities."

Both of these categories are growing faster than spending on actual necessities, which are expected to grow around 5 percent a year, about the same as expected GDP growth. Basically, discretionary categories are showing the fastest growth.

Finally, an important related issue is the Chinese tradition of saving. If you compare spending and saving rates across the emerging markets, you see a spike in savings in China. That spike is fairly understandable.

First, it's cultural. Second, they are precautionary savings—no social safety net means if you get sick, it's all on you. Third, Chinese savings are not unique. Japan, Korea, and Taiwan all hit 30-percent-plus savings rates in their early development. And fourth, without much of a consumer-finance system, it's tough to use debt to hit truly spectacular consumption levels. After all, a vacation home or car may cost the equivalent of a year's income.

That's a rant on China's macro consumer situation. Basically, it remains a great story. It may be volatile. It's also somewhat unpredictable. But you just don't get a consumer growth story this good anywhere else.

Two Brief Asides

Ok. This has been quite a bit of business-heavy content. Just for a breather, here are two totally unrelated articles on Prince Alwaleed and Warren Buffett.

HOW I WENT FROM NYC TO WORKING FOR PRINCE ALWALEED

By Jeffrey Towson

Alternate title: **How My Boss's Motivational Talk Convinced Me to Quit**

I often get asked how I ended going from New York management consulting to working for Prince Alwaleed in the Middle East. It was a pretty big career move. But it was actually a more of a gut decision. And I think there is a good (or at least interesting) career lesson in it.

Here's the story:

I joined Booz-Allen's New York office after medical school. It was my first business job and management consulting was a good way to get some training. And for 2-3 years, doing financial services in Manhattan was a good, if not exactly thrilling, experience.

But by year three, I was having misgivings. I liked the people I worked with but there was a blandness to life at big client service firms which didn't suit me. Lots of client project churn. Not much thrill. I generally prefer being in small groups (20-50) of aggressive people. And I don't like wearing a suit very much.

Then one day the global CEO of Booz-Allen came to meet the New York office. And he gave a motivational speech that convinced me to quit.

It was a corporate event at 101 Park Avenue (the same building George Costanza worked at in Seinfeld and which Captain America crashes into in the Avengers). We all filed down to the big conference room. And after some food, the CEO arrived and took the podium. He thanked us for coming and said he wanted to talk about the company and its future.

Then he did something which I have never forgotten. He said he thought he had expressed himself better at a previous event. So instead of talking to us, we should just watch a video of his past talk. He then left the stage, sat down in the audience with us and the staff put on a video of him speaking.

For the next +20 minutes, we (the client staff, the admin staff and the CEO) all sat and watched a video of him giving a motivational talk at some other event.

That was the moment I decided to quit. Actually, the thought running through my head was "this is the dumbest thing I have ever seen".

The video ended with a shot of an eagle flying and some cheesy music (something to do with flying high in life). The CEO got back up on stage and took some questions. He then left for the DC office. I went back up to my office and began planning my exit.

A quick aside.

There is often-repeated Warren Buffett advice that you should do what you love in life. If you do, you will be more effective and you will never really work a day in your life.

I think this is completely true. But I also think most people don't really have work they love that much. I certainly didn't at that point in my life. So what do you do if you haven't yet found something you really love to do?

My best answer to this (and my frequent advice to my students) is, absent loving your work, you should go work for the best and brightest people you can find. It will make you smarter. And it will put you in situations with lots of opportunities (the best people all tend to know each other). Absent knowing what you love, working for the best and brightest is a good default strategy.

Listening to the CEO that day, I realized I was neither doing a job I loved nor working for the best and brightest. Hence my spur of the moment decision to quit.

That thought was 80% of how I ended up moving to the Middle East and working for Prince Alwaleed. He was a client so there was a relationship. And I just jumped from a consulting engagement to some short-term work for him directly (looking at a struggling hospital). It was a leap of faith really. I exited my likely partner track in New York for a 3-4 month contract in Riyadh.

I decided I wanted to work for the best of the best. That was it. And I didn't care where in the world I had to go to do that or under what circumstances. At that time, Alwaleed was the world's fourth richest person. And he had turned $30k into $31B using just his brain and a phone. That was proof enough for me to take the leap. I took the 3 month contract and moved from New York to the Middle East. That initial project grew into 8-9 years of work.

And, thankfully, after several years at the center of the Alwaleed whirlwind, I had my Warren Buffett "do what you love" epiphany. I found that doing healthcare and consumer investments - and writing and teaching about it was my thing (Note: I wrote this article in Nairobi, Bangkok and Beijing). Now I study the great global investors (Alwaleed, Jorge Lemann, etc.) and then do a smaller, healthcare version of it. It fascinates me. I virtually never stop thinking about my topics. And per Warren Buffett, I have not really worked a day since.

I APPLIED WARREN BUFFETT'S 25-5 RULE TO MY CAREER - AND IT TOTALLY WORKED.

By Jeffrey Towson

Alternate Headline: "I Applied Warren Buffett's 25-5 Rule - and Now I Am Trying to Date Jessica Alba."

Warren Buffett's 25-5 rule came out of advice he gave to his airline pilot Mike Flint. The story (which may not be 100% true) is that he advised Mike to make a list of his 25 career goals. And then to circle his 5 biggest ones.

However, the point of the exercise was not really to identify the top five. It was to identify the other 20. Because these are your real problem. These are the things you like enough that you will get drawn into them. These are the things that will pull focus and time away from your top 5. These are your biggest professional distractions.

The goal of the 25-5 rule is to focus more on your top 5 goals by saying "no" to the other 20.

So I did the exercise a few months ago and it really worked. And then I took the exercise a bit too far because I tend to do that. Here is my final list.

Goal 1: Become a top global healthcare investor.

This is my biggest professional goal. It's pretty ambitious but I typically spend 6-8 hours a day doing nothing but reading healthcare (and consumer product) annual reports. I have been slowly working my way through the financials of every public healthcare company on the planet.

Goal 2: Write a classic investment book.

The goal is a book that is essential reading for business professionals and MBA students. I've published three books and +100 articles thus far. I am now making my first serious attempt at writing a classic book. It will be about the investment strategies of Prince Alwaleed. We'll see how it goes.

Goal 3: Speak at Davos / World Economic Forum

I'm not really sure how I'm going to pull this one off. But it's a one-time goal. So if I can achieve it, it will also free up a spot in my top five.

Goal 4: Exercise 3x a week - forever.

I'm at the age where I need to exercise perpetually. So this is really a goal about consistency. However, I do notice that when I exercise regularly, I become much more disciplined in other parts of my life, especially work. Per Charles Duhigg's The Power of Habits, exercising is my keystone habit.

Goal 5: Avoid the common, catastrophic screw-ups.

This goal is pretty easy to achieve as it's just stuff not to do. I keep a list of the most common catastrophic mistakes people seem to make. These are the mistakes that seem to frequently wreck otherwise successful people's lives.

My current "avoid at all costs" list includes doing drugs, gambling, having significant and/or short-term debt, going to jail, and doing overly dangerous activities (hang gliding, etc.).

* * *

Ok. Now on to the other 20 goals, which is really the point of the article.

Goal 6: Practice medicine.

I went into business right after medical school and I still think about going back to clinical practice in some form. I feel the pull of this all the time.

But practicing medicine would require a ton of time and focus. And dabbling in clinical practice is a pretty bad idea in terms of quality care. So being a doctor is now my biggest "no, don't do it" goal.

Goal 7: Launch a CalTech-type math and engineering school.

This is another long-time, big dream. I spent time at Harvey Mudd College and loved it. Ever since, I have thought about developing a college that is 100% dedicated to math and the hard sciences. This is my top contender for moving up into the top five. But for now, it's on the "no" list.

Goal 8: Sit on company boards.

I like being on Boards. It's fun and you meet great people so saying "no" here is disappointing. But it's probably smart as Board members seem to get sued all the time.

Goal 9: Write a TV show.

I have written and pitched several TV shows. No idea why I do this as business writing doesn't make very good entertainment. Putting this on the "no" list is long overdue.

* * *

Ok, thus far this exercise has been pretty logical. And it was pretty helpful. I finally said no to things that had been lingering in my mind for years.

However, I am now also out of big goals. So I started just looking at other things in my life that could be cut out. And as I have a puritanical streak, this is where I kinda went off the rails.

Goal 10: Politics.

I used to follow political stuff and go to Washington DC for meetings and such. It was pretty fun. Lots of lunches and steak houses. Plus healthcare tends to be government-infused.

But looking back, I think it was a waste of time and emotionally unhealthy for me. So I'm now completely out of this world. I don't follow political news, events, or elections. To quote the American philosopher William Joel, "I've passed the age of consciousness and righteous rage."

Goal or Activity 11: Doing intro meetings.

This is more of an activity than a goal. But I have really stopped doing casual hello meetings (professional, not personal). These meetings do add up in terms of time. I now usually say no (politely) unless there is a project on the table.

Goal or Activity 12: Following the news.

News and current events used to be the first thing I checked in the morning. But I think this soaks up too much time so I've cut it out. Plus I'm not convinced reading the news doesn't make you kinda stupid. So now, outside of the financial press, I've stopped following the news entirely. I find I don't miss it at all.

Goal or Activity 13: Expensive meals and nice hotels.

As I'm just randomly cutting stuff out of my life, I decided nice hotels and restaurants should go as well. Simple living really suits me better. And I've had enough pricey wine and chicken Ceasar salads for one lifetime. I am now a contented patron of Motel 6 and Denny's.

Activity 14: Social media. I've mostly stopped WeChat, WhatsApp, Line, Twitter, Facebook and all the rest. This has freed up a lot of time. I now really only use LinkedIn, which I think is awesome for writing.

Activity 15: Unscheduled phone calls. I'm also avoiding unscheduled phone calls and it has made a significant difference in my schedule. I schedule most calls in advance - and they need a purpose.

Activity 16: Television. Being able to flip through +500 channels is just too tempting for me. I don't own a TV anymore.

Activity 17: Video games and web surfing. Same as 16. Although I find I really miss Call of Duty.

* * *

Ok, I kinda morphed an exercise in goal prioritization into a self-righteous purge. And unfortunately, I'm still 7 goals short of 25. So to end the article, I thought I should dream up a few new goals for my life. They can be alternates for the top five.

Goal 18: Start a healthcare PE fund in Africa. I think it's too early in the development of African healthcare for this. But I just really like the idea. I'm saving this goal for my next life.

Goal 19: Get an apartment in Leblon, Rio de Janeiro. When I'm depressed, I look at real estate listings in this little Rio neighborhood.

Goal 20: Date Jessica Alba. Ok, now I'm in fantasy land. But it's the end of the article and I'm tired.

Goal 21: Hang out with Conor McGregor in Dublin. Same but for some reason I think this one is actually doable.

Goal 22-25: I'm completely out of ideas.

Overall, Buffett's 25-5 rule has been a big help. Especially in forcing me to let go of some long-standing dreams. The top 10 list was pretty helpful. I'm not sure the rest of the list helped that much. It was mostly just me being maniacal.

I recommend giving 25-5 a try, but maybe stop at 15.

* * *

Ok. These two articles were just a quick aside and a bit of a break. Now back to our four contrarian points about China.

POINT III
CHINA CAN INNOVATE BIG TIME

The "China can't innovate" and "Chinese can only copy" stereotypes have never really been true. After all, China invented gunpowder, printing, paper-making and the compass among other things. But at the beginning of China's forced march into the global markets in the 1980s, its technology was sadly way behind. Decades of isolation with no one but the Soviet Union to rely on (before you kick them out) will do that to you.

So what has been happening is China has been playing catch-up with regards to technology. Importing foreign technology has been a major part of this. For example, Foreign Direct Investment has been running at about $70 billion per annum for decades. In automotive, telecom equipment, chemicals, and many other sectors foreign investors have been the cornerstone for technological development. This importing phenomenon has tended to reinforce the "China can't innovate" stereotype.

However, our experience has been that Chinese companies are exceedingly clever. And they innovate like crazy. For example, Chinese patents grew by 46% in 2016 according to the World

Intellectual Property Organization putting it on track to overtake the US and Japan. While these patent numbers can be a bit suspect (and quality varies), the domestic patent office still handles over 1 million applications a year, making it by far the busiest in the world. Also, China now spends more on R&D than any other country in the world except the US (over $200 billion in 2015). And China has more than 29,000 PhDs graduating each and every year. Across the board, the pure volume of innovation-type activity in China is staggering.

One issue is that a lot of this innovation-type activity has been focused on industries where cost innovation and customer-facing innovation are key. This tends to not be considered the same as innovation in science and engineering. But in industries like video gaming, consumer electronics, machine tools and polyester fibre, China achieves more than its fair share of global value-added.

In science and engineering, the record is more mixed. For example, China still doesn't really have its own car company. But on the other hand, China already makes more than 80 percent of the world's high speed rail, over 30 percent of its wind turbines, and has the only strong smart grid in the world.

And this is not even the really cool part. The cool part is that China is not just starting to create insanely great products and services, it is also changing how innovation happens globally. Prototypes can be developed 5 times as fast in Shenzhen as in Silicon Valley. Research and manufacturing talent in China is available at 10 to 30 percent of global cost. And in Chinese cities you can now find every MNC in the world doing research. For example, in Shanghai 7 out of 10 of the world's largest pharma MNCs now have R&D

centers. So yes, China can innovate big time. In fact, China is making innovation itself cheaper, faster and more global.

In this section, we present nine essays that discuss China's growing ability to innovate - and to change how innovation happens globally.

CHINA IS WAY MORE INNOVATIVE THAN YOU THINK

By Jonathan Woetzel

The events of 2015 and 2016 have shown that China is passing through a challenging transition: the labor-force expansion and surging investment that propelled three decades of growth are now weakening. This is a natural step in the country's economic development. Yet it raises questions such as how drastically the expansion of GDP will slow down and whether the country can tap new sources of growth.

Research by the McKinsey Global Institute (MGI) suggests that to realize consensus growth forecasts—5.5 to 6.5 percent a year—during the coming decade, China must generate two to three percentage points of annual GDP growth through innovation, broadly defined. If it does, innovation could contribute much of the required $3 trillion to $5 trillion a year of annual incremental GDP by 2025.

This means China will have evolved from an "innovation sponge" - absorbing and adapting existing technology and knowledge from around the world - into a global innovation leader. McKinsey analysis suggests that this transformation is possible, though far from inevitable.

To date, when Chinese companies have commercialized new ideas and used them to raise market share and profits, the picture has been decidedly mixed. In areas such as consumer electronics and construction equipment, China has become a strong innovator.

Yet in others such as creating new drugs and designing automobile engines, the country still isn't globally competitive. That's true even though every year it spends more than $350 billion on research (second only to the United States), turns out close to 30,000 PhDs in science and engineering, and leads the world in patent applications (more than 1 million in 2015).

Looking ahead, there are broad swaths of opportunity. McKinsey analysis suggests that by 2025, new innovation opportunities could contribute $1.0 trillion to $2.2 trillion a year to the Chinese economy.

To achieve this goal, China must continue to transform the manufacturing sector, particularly through digitization, and the service sector, through rising connectivity and Internet enablement. Additional productivity gains could come from progress in science- and engineering-based innovations and improvements in the operations of companies.

To develop a clearer view of this potential, it is useful to define four innovation archetypes: customer focused, efficiency driven, engineering based, and science based.

Chinese companies that rely on customer-focused and efficiency-driven innovation—in industries such as household appliances, Internet software and services, solar panels, and construction machinery—perform relatively well. Many of the most successful Chinese companies excel in these areas.

However, Chinese companies are not yet global leaders in any of the science-based industries (such as branded pharmaceuticals) that were analyzed.

In engineering-based industries, the results are inconsistent. China excels in high-speed trains but gets less than its GDP-based share from auto manufacturing.

The following is a summary of the outlook for innovation in these four categories, starting with the two outperformers.

1. CUSTOMER-FOCUSED INNOVATION: THE CHINESE COMMERCIALIZATION MACHINE

China benefits from the sheer size of its consumer market, which helps companies to commercialize new ideas quickly and on a large scale. Even a relatively small market like online gaming is bigger than the auto industry in Turkey or Thailand. Chinese companies have learned how to read the requirements of their rapidly urbanizing country and to scale up new products and services quickly to meet them.

Manufacturers of appliances and other household goods dominated the first wave of customer-focused innovation in China. These innovations were "good enough" products such as refrigerators and TV sets. But these offerings no longer suffice to gain a growing share of consumers.

Companies like smartphone manufacturer Xiaomi, Oppo and Vivo are responding with cheaper and better products designed to offer hardware features as good as those from global brands but priced for the Chinese market. Like other customer-focused innovators in China, Xiaomi uses the massive consumer market as a collaborator, rapidly refining its offerings through online feedback.

Internet service providers are another hotbed of customer-focused innovation. Alibaba, Baidu, and Tencent have become global leaders in online services, largely thanks to their success in the enormous Chinese market.

2. EFFICIENCY-DRIVEN INNOVATION: THE ECOSYSTEM ADVANTAGE

In manufacturing, China's extensive ecosystem has provided an unmatched environment for efficiency-driven innovation. The country has the world's largest and most highly concentrated supplier base, a massive manufacturing workforce, and a modern logistics infrastructure. These advantages give Chinese manufacturers a lead in some important knowledge-based manufacturing categories, such as electrical equipment, construction equipment, and solar panels.

The challenges are mounting, however. As wages rise, the country becomes less competitive for the most labor-intensive work. At the same time, a worldwide transition is under way toward a new kind of manufacturing, sometimes called Industry 4.0: a much more intense digital linkage of manufacturing components, processes, and logistics.

As a result, Chinese companies will face pressure to improve their performance in utilizing assets, matching supply with demand, and controlling quality.

Entrepreneurs are poised to play a bigger role in this area. In Shenzhen, a rich ecosystem of component suppliers, design services, business incubators, and outsourced assembly capacity has helped start-ups prototype products and scale up global manufacturing businesses quickly.

3. ENGINEERING-BASED INNOVATION IN 'LEARNING INDUSTRIES'

China has had mixed success with engineering-based innovation. The best performers are found in Chinese markets where motivated domestic industries are nurtured by national and local governments that create local demand, push for innovation, and facilitate the transfer of knowledge from foreign players. China has used this formula successfully in high-speed rail (Chinese companies have a 41 percent share of the global railroad-equipment revenues, according to McKinsey estimates), wind power, and telecommunications equipment.

Learning and innovation have been slower to come in automotive manufacturing. To date, most domestic Chinese carmakers have relied on platforms from their global partners or on designs from outside firms to bring products to market quickly. Thanks to exploding domestic demand and strong profit streams from joint ventures, they have felt little pressure to innovate.

In other industries, such as medical equipment, the private sector will drive innovation. Mindray, United Imaging Healthcare, and other smaller Chinese players will continue to make inroads in market categories (for instance, CT scanners and MRI machines) that foreign suppliers now dominate.

4. SCIENCE-BASED INNOVATION: NOVEL CHINESE APPROACHES

A massive government push to raise R&D spending, train more scientists, and file more patents has yet to give China a lead in science-based innovation. This slow progress has a number of explanations—not least that this type of work takes a long time to pay off and requires an effective regulator to protect intellectual property.

Huge investments by government and the private sector to shepherd projects from the lab to commercial deployment are needed, as well. What's more, despite the large number of Chinese students trained in scientific and technical fields, companies struggle to find capable talent.

Chinese innovators are adopting novel approaches—for instance, using the country's massive market size and huge pool of low-cost researchers to industrialize and speed up experimentation and data collection. One such innovator, BeiGene, gained ground in the biotech industry by developing drugs to treat cancers and other diseases. The company has accelerated the drug-discovery process by deploying a large-scale drug-testing team, testing compounds on human tissue (such as cancerous tumor samples) during the preclinical phase to get early indications of issues that might arise in human testing, and capitalizing on access to China's large pool of patients

The extent and speed of China's advances in innovation will have significant implications for the country's growth and competitiveness and for the types of jobs, products, and services available to the Chinese people. They will also have powerful consequences for multinationals (competing at home and abroad with Chinese companies), some of which are now using China as an R&D base for global innovation.

Fortunately, that isn't a zero-sum game: a more innovative China ought to be good for a global economy that seeks new sources of growth.

HOW THE INTERNET IS SHAKING UP CHINA'S BANKING SECTOR

By Jonathan Woetzel

Increasing online competition in the banking sector is shaking up traditionally staid business models around the world. But for Chinese banks – already struggling to adapt to liberalization – this shift is turning out to be seismic, as the country's institutions face a wave of competition from internet finance companies that is changing the industry landscape.

Where existing banks have legacy systems and processes, companies emerging from the technology side have the advantages of agility and deep technical talent. Now they are quickly building the financial capabilities to compete head-to-head with traditional financial institutions.

The Chinese government has announced a pilot program of banks owned entirely by private companies such as Alibaba and Tencent, as it steps up liberalization of its financial sector. Tencent is one of the participants in Webank, which will focus on lending to small firms and consumers. The official entry into the banking sector of online groups further blurs the boundary between internet companies and financial institutions.

With competition heating up, banks are under greater pressure than ever to increase their online offerings. Chinese consumers hold roughly 60 per cent of their personal financial assets in bank deposits (far above the 12 per cent held by US consumers). But as the internet lowers the minimum threshold for investing while improving financial literacy and convenience, customers are diversifying their portfolios.

In June 2013, Alipay launched Yu'ebao; just a year later, its assets under management had swelled to about RMB 570 billion, making it the largest money market fund in China and the fourth-largest in the world. Yu'ebao's success has spurred competitors such as Baidu and Tencent to follow suit with similar offerings.

As consumers move away from bank deposits toward other asset management products, however, they are largely doing so via websites such as Yu'ebao or online discount brokerages that produce lower margins.

Chinese banks, securities firms, and insurance companies have already built online channels for distribution, marketing, and transactions – and Chinese consumers have been quick to shift with them.

The Securities Association of China found that 98 per cent of customers at securities firms have registered for online accounts. Meanwhile, the Industrial and Commercial Bank of China estimates an online transaction is typically one-seventh the cost of a transaction at a branch counter.

But while the move to online channels lowers transaction costs, it requires investment and erodes margins by empowering consumers to compare products, fees and interest rates. China's banks and financial firms will have to counter this effect by using their online channels to become more efficient in sales and marketing and to reach previously unreachable customers.

Beyond the customer-facing side, it is critical also to update back-office and logistics functions to streamline and cut costs. Big data analytics could provide an answer to one of the biggest problems looming over China's banking sector: a rising tide of non-performing loans.

Ecommerce platforms typically own a huge amount of information on both small merchants and consumers, including payment histories, point-of-sale data, stock levels, and social network activity. With the right capabilities, banks can analyze this information to reduce risk and increase lending to the underserved small businesses and retail segments.

In addition to providing banks with credit information, some ecommerce companies – including Alibaba and JD – have established their own micro-lending arms.

China's banks and financial firms will face increasing talent shortages, particularly for highly specialized roles in big data analytics, and some may opt to increase their skills pool through acquisitions or partnerships.

What is clear is that institutions willing to embrace these changes and stay at the forefront of innovation have the potential to capture enormous value. Research from the McKinsey Global Institute projects that by 2025 Chinese banks could save some RMB 800 billion each year by using big data analytics to reduce non-performing loans and another RMB 230 billion by moving more of their operations online.

But the potential ripple effects beyond the banking sector are even larger. Better allocation of capital to small and medium-sized enterprises could add 1 to 2 percentage points to China's overall GDP growth from now until 2025, creating up to 11 million jobs.

CHINA'S RESOURCE BOOM: IT'S NOT WHAT YOU THINK IT IS

By Jonathan Woetzel

China has recently said it would scrap plans to build 85 coal plants and instead invest $350 billion in renewables. This is just one of many ways technology is reshaping the world of resources and transforming the global economy in the process. And China is at the center of it.

Technological innovation— including the adoption of robotics, Internet of Things technology, and data analytics are changing consumer behavior and fundamentally transforming the way resources are consumed and produced.

China is playing a key role in this transformation as it:

- Shifts to more service and consumption led growth
- Invests heavily in renewables
- Transitions away from a dependence on fossil fuels

And China will do this at the same time as it accounts for a growing share of global energy demand.

According to new research at the McKinsey Global Institute, the growth of primary energy demand will slow and could even peak in 2025 if new technologies are adopted rapidly. Demand for oil and coal will also likely peak and could decline over the next two decades. Less intensive use of energy and increased efficiency could potentially raise energy productivity in the global economy by between 40 to 70 percent in the same period.

But while overall global energy demand slows, China's share of that demand is growing. By 2035, China could account for 28 percent of the world's primary energy demand up from 24 percent today. In comparison, the United States could account for 12 percent of global energy demand in 2035, a decline from 16 percent today. That means in this new commodities era, China dominates the resource market, accounting for more than double the share of demand coming from the US.

China's rapid industrialization, its urbanization on a massive scale, and its surging economic growth were the primary factors that drove up prices during the 2003-2015 commodities supercycle. By 2015, China was consuming more than half of the global supply of iron ore and thermal coal and about 40 percent of the world's copper. Then came the end of the supercycle, in part driven by a shift within China, as it began transitioning from an investment driven economic model to a services and consumption led one, and reduced its appetite for additional resources.

Today, **China is helping to drive a global trend in declining resource intensity**. Increased energy efficiency in residential, industrial and commercial buildings, lower demand for energy from transport due to the rise of electric and autonomous vehicles and ride sharing, together with the falling costs and greater penetration of renewables will reduce global consumption of resources.

China has already made significant progress in reducing the resource intensity of its economy and plans to do more. While China's economy grew 18 fold from 1980 to 2010, energy consumption grew only five fold. Energy intensity per unit of China's GDP declined 70 percent during this period, according to the World Bank. And the Chinese government aims to reduce energy intensity by 15 percent in its 13th five-year plan, from 2016 to 2020, after targeting a 20 percent reduction in the period 2006 to 2010 and a 12 percent reduction from 2011 to 2015.

Renewables are one factor behind declining resource intensity. They are not only substitutes for fossil fuels, but also reduce overall demand for energy, as they do not incur the heat losses associated with fossil fuel power generation. As solar and wind continue to become cheaper with the deployment of new technology, renewables will play a substantially larger role in the global economy's energy mix.

If costs continue to fall at the current pace, solar and wind energy could be competitive by 2025, without subsidies, with the marginal cost of thermal coal or natural gas generation in most regions globally. Renewables could grow from 4 percent of power generation today to as much as 36 percent of global electricity supply by 2035, our research shows.

China is investing heavily in renewables with ambitions to be a world leader. Currently, China invests more than $100 billion a year in domestic renewables, double the amount that the United States invests domestically. In addition, China is investing $32 billion overseas, more than any other country, and China's State Grid Corporation announced plans to develop a global grid that draws on wind turbines and solar panels from around the world.

China's top tier companies are gaining leadership across renewable value chains. For example, China's solar panel manufacturers are estimated in recent studies to have about a 20 percent cost advantage compared with US peers thanks to economies of scale and supply chain developments. Chinese wind turbine manufacturers have been gradually closing technology gaps and now account for over 90 percent of the domestic market, up from just 25 percent in 2002.

So not only will China be the biggest center of demand in the world but will also be the source of cutting edge technology. And that means China has a unique opportunity to provide a leadership role. Its experience in reducing the energy intensity of its economy can provide a way forward for other developing nations. And its development of renewables at home and abroad can lead to further technological breakthroughs and drive costs lower, benefitting consumers of energy everywhere. Indeed, China seems to be taking a more active leadership role on energy. Just last month Chinese

President Xi Jinping urged the United States and the world to stick to hard won agreements on climate change.

But China faces challenges in its transition from fossil fuels to renewables and from the overall transformation of the global resource sector. For starters, it is still highly dependent on coal and will face sizeable costs as its shifts capacity from coal to other resources like natural gas and renewables. At the same time, its construction of solar panels and wind farms have outpaced upgrades to the electrical grid, creating a great deal of waste. And its producers, like others around the world, face increasing pressure to drive costs down and increase efficiencies in an era of slower global demand for commodities.

Technological advances should ease some of these pressures, particularly for producers. Automated hauling trucks, underwater robots that can fix gas pipelines, drones that conduct predictive maintenance on wind turbines, data analytics that can improve outcomes across operations, these and other technological developments can help producers drive down costs and increase efficiency.

Just as technology helps producers unlock productivity gains, it will help consumers unlock savings from lower consumption of resources. We calculate total cost savings from both changes to the supply and demand for major commodities could be substantial, somewhere between $900 billion and $1.6 trillion in 2035 for the global economy, an amount equivalent to the GDP of Indonesia or, at the higher end of our range, the GDP of Canada.

How big these savings end up being will depend not just on how quickly new technology is adopted but on how policymakers and companies adapt to their new environment. More and more though, it will also depend on China.

HOW TMALL BECAME A MIDWIFE FOR CHINESE CROSS-BORDER M&A

By Jeffrey Towson

In recent years, Taobao, Tmall and other online shopping sites have created a new way for Chinese consumers to buy foreign goods directly online. This new sales channel, commonly known as *haitao*, has, unsurprisingly, produced a surge in purchases of vitamins, milk powder and other products Chinese have already been buying on trips overseas.

What is surprising is that this new online channel also appears to be catalyzing Chinese merger and acquisition activity overseas. Small and medium-sized foreign companies that show strong online sales to Chinese consumers are becoming ideal acquisition targets for Chinese companies. Suddenly, being ranked among the top sellers on Tmall International is raising the likelihood that a Chinese company will come calling.

Consider the sale of Swisse Wellness Group, one of Australia's leading vitamin and supplement companies. Founded in 1969, Swisse has traditionally sold vitamins, health products, minerals and supplements through local pharmacies, health food stores, supermarkets and clinics. It has a market share of about 18% in Australia.

During the first half of 2015, something strange happened. Swisse abruptly found its sales into China growing rapidly, both via tourists and through the emerging haitao channel. Revenues for the year that ended in June 2015 reportedly climbed to 313 million Australian dollars ($228 million) from A$126 million a year earlier.

But Swisse had not actually launched any major initiatives to tap into the Chinese market. In fact, its China success was probably a surprise to management. The company was simply doing what it had always done: selling in Australia through its normal distributors and channels.

What was happening was that Chinese distributors and other haitao intermediaries had begun buying Swisse products in bulk and were putting them up for sale on Tmall and Taobao. Swisse Vitamin was suddenly the No. 1 brand by transaction volume on both Tmall and Taobao for the 6 months through March 2015, leapfrogging over global brands such as Amway and General Nutrition's GNC.

The lesson here is when 1.3 billion Chinese consumers get interested in a small company it can really move the needle financially. Swisse's online sales in China and to Chinese tourists in Australia jumped to about 30% of its revenue and 50% of its earnings before interest, taxes, depreciation and amortization.

And that brings us to Tmall's emerging role as the midwife of Chinese M&A. Swisse's cross-border buying surge caught the interest of major Chinese private equity firms and strategic buyers. Suddenly, Swisse appeared to be an ideal acquisition target. Not only was it a small foreign company with a trusted brand -- vital in health products -- it also now had proven China sales and the potential for much greater growth in the country.

By mid-year, privately-held Swisse was in play. And in September, Biostime International Holdings, a Hong Kong-listed producer of infant formula and baby care products, bought an 83% stake for A$1.39 billion. Biostime has said it will distribute Swisse's products across China and through more e-commerce channels.

Such haitao-driven acquisitions seem particularly well suited to South Korea and Australia. In Australia, there are already lots of Chinese nationals and word-of-mouth is critical for online sales in China. Additionally, Australian brands are widely trusted, not a small thing in food and supplements in China. For Australian companies, this situation also works quite well. Most have limited growth opportunities at home and lack the ability to expand to China directly on their own.

We are also starting to see this show up in the U.S. Natural Health Trends, a Texas-based multi-level marketing company for health and wellness products, is now generating approximately 80% of its revenue through e-commerce channels into Hong Kong and China. Its annual revenues soared from $52.5 million in 2013 to $124.6 million in 2014.

Ultimately, this Tmall midwife phenomenon is about Chinese consumers becoming increasingly numerous and wealthy. And they are going to get what they want, one way or the other. This all augurs well for small foreign companies with good consumer products and trusted brands.

(re-printed with permission from the Nikkei Asian Review, located here)

APPLE'S ACHILLES' HEEL IN CHINA IS RAPIDLY IMPROVING LOCAL APPS AND SERVICES

By Jeffrey Towson

Apple's success in China has been spectacular. Truly outstanding. But while the "Apple in China" story is usually told in terms of the rise (and now leveling off) of iPhone sales, it has also been just as big a success in terms of brand building and customer capture.

Apple today is known and loved by China's increasingly wealthy urban middle class. And the company has a commanding position in the lucrative "affordable luxury" market segment. Apple's success in rising consumer China is even better than its growth numbers imply.

However... (you knew it was coming)

While capturing Chinese consumers has been a big accomplishment, the critical question now is "can they keep them?" And a big part of the answer – and their biggest risk going forward I think – is whether or not they can address their lack of services and software in China.

I will expand on this with the below points - and then I will propose a few potential solutions:

POINT 1: APPLE IS WELL-POSITIONED IN ONE OF CHINA'S MOST ATTRACTIVE MARKET NICHES, "AFFORDABLE LUXURY".

Affordable luxury in China is not selling BMW cars or fine art, which are still beyond the means of the vast majority of the population. Affordable luxury is Coach bags, vacations to Thailand and new iPhones, not the refurbished or fake ones.

These types of purchases are not that pricey and are rapidly becoming affordable for much of China's populace. They are also directly benefiting from the transition of urban consumers from bargain-hunting buyers of life's basics into more emotional and loyal consumers. Sellers of affordable luxury products and services can not only command premium prices, they can also benefit from the steadily increasing disposable income of urban households.

The sale of iPhones to Chinese consumers, and this demographic in particular, has resulted in surging growth for Apple over the past five years. China is now the company's third-largest market by revenue (2016). China was also the source of half the company's growth. All the while, gross margins have remained around 40% globally. This is fairly amazing. OnePlus co-founder Carl Pei recently speculated that 90% of the profits in smartphones were probably going to Apple.

However, analysts have increasingly been discussing a plateauing of iPhones sales in China. I think these comments miss an important point that the iPhone remains very expensive in China relative to average income levels. iPhones are still in the process of becoming affordable to a wider base of consumers, so the trend line remains attractive.

Additionally, Apple's unique position in Chinese affordable luxury creates an important side benefit in application development. While Apple's iOS operating system may be dwarfed in the Chinese market by Google's Android (like 85% is Android), Apple has the customers who will actually spend money to buy apps and add features. This means Apple gets extensive developer attention in China, beyond its actual market share.

POINT 2: UNFORTUNATELY, THE SMARTPHONE MARKET OF CHINA IS GETTING MUCH MORE DIFFICULT.

There is a lot of pessimism about smartphones in China recently. I'm just going to skim through this as it's pretty standard stuff. Feel free to skip to Point 3.

After years of rapid growth, flatlining sales are resulting in a painful shake-out.

There was a 5% contraction in smartphone sales in the first quarter of 2016 (Strategy Analytics). And there was slippage by companies such as Apple and Xiaomi.

And as this comes after five years of stellar growth, there is likely a post-boom shake-out happening. Smaller players are expected to exit or consolidate (especially if they only make phones). OnePlus has announced layoffs. And many smartphone suppliers are in trouble. Several have gone bankrupt and FIH mobile warned of a 92% drop in first half year 2016 profits.

Chinese smartphone companies are dominating - and moving upscale.

Go back to 2011 and 70% of the smartphones in China were foreign (mostly Samsung, Apple and Nokia). Today the market is dominated by Chinese phone makers. Apple is really only one of 2-3 foreign smartphone makers still alive in the Mainland. And unfortunately for Apple and Samsung, the Chinese are now moving upscale into premium phones.

No barriers to entry for basic smart phones.

The situation is even worse in discount smartphones. It is getting easier and easier to enter this business. Xiaomi showed that by going from a start-up to a big success in three years. Oppo and OnePlus have both entered in the last couple years and have risen quickly.

We are now even seeing "micro runs", in which local companies are creating and selling batches of 20,000-30,000 phones with an office and just a few staff. So the competition in cheap smartphones is getting more intensive, while the premium market is being invaded.

* * *

Against this worsening situation, I think Apple is still mostly staying above the fray. As mentioned, they have captured a huge number of particularly valuable Chinese customers. They do have a unique brand and reputation. And premium smartphones do require constant upgrades and technological advances, for which Apple deploys $10B in R&D annually in R&D and does frequent technology acquisitions.

So I give Apple the benefit of doubt that they will likely stay at the frontier technologically. And in China, I do think they have, to some degree, what Warren Buffett calls a "share of the consumer mind". The iPhone is the quality phone to have in China today. And Apple can keep reinforcing this with their massive marketing spend and their fantastic China stores.

But my main point is that selling smartphones without services is a very difficult game in China. And going forward, this market and Apple's position look increasingly at risk – mostly because they lack the stickiness of software and services that they enjoy in the West.

POINT 3: APPLE IN CHINA IS EXPOSED. THEY LARGELY LACK THE SERVICES, SOFTWARE AND PLATFORMS THAT GIVE THEM COMPETITIVE PROTECTION AND CUSTOMER RETENTION IN THE WEST.

In China, Apple basically sells hardware - lots of iPhones and some iPads. And other companies, mostly Chinese, populate them with services and software. Apple in China largely lacks the services and platforms that give it competitive protection and "customer stickiness" in the West.

Chinese iPhone users simply do not worry about losing movies or music purchased from Apple should they change brands. Nor do they worry about losing friends in iMessenger or files stored in iCloud. They are mostly not using those Apple services.

Software and platforms can create network effects and other switching costs that protect Apple from the unpredictability of successfully developing and selling a cool new smartphone model every year or two. And they create a buying relationship on a daily or weekly basis.

Without software and services in China, there is no real guarantee that Apple can keep the valuable Chinese customers it has so successfully captured. Consider the chaotic shifts in market position over the past years that have seen Nokia, Samsung Electronics and Xiaomi each rise to the top before falling.

In economist-terminology, Apple in China doesn't have the high switching costs and network effects (both two-sided and complementary) that keep their customers from year to year. While

Apple may make $140B in iPhone sales globally, it is their +$20M in software and services that really locks in their customers.

POINT 4: APPLE IS ALSO FACING ADDITIONAL THREATS THAT ARE MORE UNIQUE TO CHINA.

The transition from touch to voice as the primary phone interface appears to be happening fast in China. This is perhaps because typing in Chinese is more difficult? And while Apple does pretty well with its Siri personal assistant in English, it is behind on Mandarin as a voice input.

One company to watch here is Baidu. It appears to be moving fast and is focused on developing high quality Mandarin recognition. If the primary interface for the iPhone in China becomes another company's Mandarin-recognition application, this would be a problem for Apple.

China has also become the world capital for mobile payments, with Tencent's WeChat commanding a particularly high level of engagement in this area. That is daunting for Apple. The politics of payments are also important and not in Apple's favor. All this will make Apple Pay's late entry into China a challenge.

POINT 5: WECHAT AND OTHER RIVAL GATEWAYS ARE A PARTICULARLY BIG THREAT.

Beyond payments, WeChat is becoming the app that contains and controls the other apps a smartphone user might want, effectively becoming an alternate homescreen. This is a direct threat to Apple's control of the user experience of Chinese iPhone owners.

Additionally, China is also now the leading market for on-demand transportation (i.e. Didi Chuxing). And this service incorporates mapping, payment systems and other commonly used services. Apple's recent investment in Didi is interesting and could bring them into this space. But the deal does not appear to have any operational tie-ins yet.

* * *

Thus, in service after service, Apple is being outrun in China's innovative mobile world. This is reducing it more and more to a pure hardware company, exactly the direction Apple does not want to go in terms of securing its current customers.

How Apple can breakthrough in China software and services

Apple today appears to be searching for entry points into China services. Its investment in May of $1 billion in Didi Chuxing can be seen as part of this. It has also been attempting to expand Apple Pay, iCloud, iTunes Movies and iBooks in China, all without too much success. Everyone in China uses Baidu for maps, WeChat for instant messaging, its affiliated Tenpay service or Alibaba Group Holding's rival Alipay for mobile payments and so on.

A big unspoken part of this is the big role of the government in these markets. Many of these services are political and the government cares who wins. The combination of fierce local competition and active state involvement is frequently fatal for foreign internet companies in China.

Apart from this, the strength of Apple in China itself is a concern for the government. The authorities are simply not going to allow Apple to have direct, uncontested control of the phones of some 200 million Chinese.

However, Apple does have options for breaking into software and services in China. And they can leverage their big strengths: an enviable reputation, a broad customer base and a huge cash pile.

One strategy would be to emulate Intel Capital's successful approach in China. This would mean investing in early-stage mobile tech and services companies across the country. The goal would be to increase the use of Apple's technology and ecosystem. Like Intel, Apple could position itself relative to other venture capital investors as an attractive, long-term partner which can provide introductions to other large tech companies and offer access to a global network of engineers, technologies and customers.

Apple could also do more Didi-type investments. They have the cash to keep buying into successful later-stage service companies. There is no reason Apple cannot do 10 more such deals. But for this to solidify its current China business, it needs an operational tie-in or technology agreement.

Another option is a larger partnership in China, say with Xiaomi. Such partnerships are how virtually all foreign media and Internet companies operate in the country. It would also give it a mainstream brand to complement its premium brand. The deal Xiaomi unveiled in 2016 with Microsoft, which includes a pledge to install Microsoft apps on Xiaomi phones, is worth watching in this regard.

* * *

Ultimately, Apple in China today is not the Apple of Tim Cook and Steve Jobs in the West. It is more like the Apple of 1982. It is a story of meteoric success but a somewhat precarious year-to-year existence based on new product launches on a rapidly shifting terrain. Deliver a great product and it's boom time, as happened with the Apple II personal computer. Deliver a dud and the dark days are back.

Services and software will be key to minimizing this volatility, securing Apple's large existing customer base and preserving its exceptional success in China. It does not need services as a new source of revenue growth as the really big money will continue to be in selling handsets. But their big China business and cash flow need better protection.

Article reposted with permission from Nikkei Asian Review, link here.

WELCOME TO THE US-CHINA PLATFORM WARS

By Jeffrey Towson

In the past year, we have seen increasing collisions between leading Chinese and Western platform businesses. For example:

- In November, Chinese travel platform Ctrip announced its acquisition of UK-based flight search engine Skyscanner. This is part of a global expansion by Ctrip, which is bringing it (again) into competition with Expedia.

- Since buying Uber China, Didi has continued its international moves – such as its investments in Indian Ola, American Lyft and SE Asian Grab.

- Jack Ma has repeatedly said that 50% of Alibaba's revenue will be international by 2025. This, plus cross-border e-commerce, is increasingly bringing them into competition with Western marketplace platforms, especially Amazon.

- Mastercard and Visa are continuing their fight with UnionPay in both China and internationally. In September, UnionPay announced that its card is now usable at 80% of US merchants and at all US atms.

- Taikang Insurance recently became the largest investor in Sotheby's. This is the latest move in the increasing competition between Chinese and Western art auction platforms (Poly and Guardian vs. Sotheby's and Christies).

- Everyone from Apple and UnionPay to Huawei and Xiaomi is jumping into e-payments, which are expanding internationally.

Powerful Chinese platform businesses are going international, usually following their Chinese customers. At the same time, powerful Western platform businesses are looking for entry points into China. So we are seeing collisions between these unique, multi-sided platform businesses. Uber vs. Didi. Airbnb vs. Tujia. Ctrip vs. Expedia. UnionPay vs. Mastercard. Alibaba vs. Amazon. We are at the beginning of what I am calling the "US-China platform wars".

This article is theory-heavy on how these types of businesses compete. It lays the foundation for the next articles. If theory is not your thing, you can skip to the next article if you want.

POINT 1: MULTI-SIDED PLATFORMS CAN HAVE BIG ADVANTAGES AGAINST TRADITIONAL COMPANIES.

Multi-sided platforms (MSPs) are different than traditional vertical merchant businesses (VIs) because they have to serve more than one user group at the same time. Instead of having one set of customers (e.g., people buying lattes or smartphones), multi-sided platforms (MSPs) serve several groups simultaneously. For example, Alibaba must serve both online buyers and sellers. Dating clubs must serve both men and women. MSPs are common in software and we can see them in operating systems, social networks, video game development, and online marketplaces. But they are also common offline. For example, credit cards, shopping malls, auction houses, and dating clubs are all MSPs.

Having multiple user groups on your platform can create certain advantages. For example:

- An MSP can use revenue from one group of users to **subsidize the prices to another group**. For example, Didi can use revenues from its drivers to decrease the prices paid by its riders. Taxi companies, without the ability to subsidize, must then compete against these lower prices. Google, Amazon, and Alibaba have all been particularly effective at horizontally entering more traditional industries with this type of subsidy approach. For example, the map industry, which relied on map sales to customers, has been devastated by Baidu and Google Maps, both of which subsidize mapping to the point of being free.

- Two-sided platforms (a MSP with two groups of users) can often wreak havoc on traditional merchant businesses (VIs). For example, eBay versus traditional retailers. However, three-sided platforms (e.g., Facebook and Google) can also often wreak havoc on two-sided platforms. For example, Facebook (which has +3 sides) can devastate advertising-supported media platforms like Yahoo and print journalism (two-sided platforms). And so on. **The more user groups you have the more options you have for pricing, offered features and bundling of features**. I've lost track of how many sides Tencent has on its platform.

- Another advantage **some MSPs have is the "network effect"**, also called demand economies of scale. Basically, each new user makes the platform more valuable to other users. This effect can be direct. For example, every person who signs up for Wechat makes the service more valuable to everyone using it because there are more people you can connect with. The effect can also be indirect. For example, every new Didi driver makes the service more valuable to every rider, but not to other drivers. And every new rider makes it more valuable to every driver, but not to other riders. But the point is that bigger platforms with a network effect actually offer tangibly better services than smaller ones. So these types of markets tend to collapse to the larger players quickly (does Wechat have a competitor in China anymore?). However, not all MSPs have a network effect. Some do and some don't. And some have but are weak and easily broken.

- Finally, MSPs can have competitive advantages even without a network effect. You can often get **economies of scale** because these types of platforms often have significant upfront and ongoing fixed costs. You have to maintain the platform regardless of how many people use it. You can also get scale in marketing expenditures.

POINT 2: TWO-SIDED NETWORKS OFTEN STRUGGLE AT THE BEGINNING WITH PRICING, FEATURES AND A "CHICKEN-AND-EGG" PROBLEM

Two-sided networks (and other MSPs) can be very difficult to launch. As mentioned, you have to serve two (or more) groups of users at the same time: both drivers and riders of private cars; both travelers and homeowners; both online sellers and buyers; both men and women (for dating platforms and local bars), and so on. And if you don't have enough of each group, the whole platform collapses to zero.

Figuring out how to get the services, features and pricing right for both sides of your platform can be difficult. Usually you charge one side more than the other. For example, bars don't charge women on ladies night. Then the men follow and you charge them more. Sony charges video game players but subsidizes video game developers. Pricing is tricky and most of the money typically comes from one side.

Additionally, each group wants different things. You need to figure out what services and features to offer. For example, eBay is offering its sellers decreased transaction costs, easy payment services, and a greater likelihood of finding a buyer. Providing each of these services costs money. Figuring out the right equation in services, features and pricing for both sides can be very difficult.

This is one of the reasons why first movers in two-sided platforms are rarely the big winners. For example, Mastercard and Visa were actually late entrants into credit cards (a two sided network). The first mover was actually the Diners Club. American Express was third. MasterCard and Visa entered quite a bit later. We will see this is a big factor in the home-sharing in China today. The equation for services and pricing still hasn't been figured out.

Finally, there is also a "chicken and egg" problem at the beginning. When Uber launched, it had to get drivers to initially sign-up. But to get them it needed to offer them lots of riders. But to get the first riders, it needed to offer them lots of drivers (and short-wait times).

It is the same for credit cards. To get merchants to initially accept your credit card (and pay 1-3%), you need to already have lots of cardholders to offer them. But to get cardholders, you need to say the card is already accepted by lots of merchants.

This is the chicken-and-egg problem. And there are lots of approaches to solving it. Usually it is by subsidizing one side and then doing a sort of zig-zag where you add some users and then some merchants and then repeat. It took Airbnb many years of struggle to get around this problem.

POINT 3: COMPLEMENTARY AND INTER-CONNECTED PLATFORMS CAN BE PARTICULARLY POWERFUL.

A single platform is good. As mentioned, it can have lots of strengths, particularly when competing against a traditional vertically integrated merchant (VI). Especially, if you can get a network effect and some economies of scale going.

But **complementary networks** can be even better. This is when you actually have two different MSPs serving a common set of users. The two MSPs can sort of amplify each other. For example, Microsoft Word (an MSP) is helped by being on the Microsoft Operating system (another MSP). They both have a user group in common and amplify each other. A mapping application (sometimes an MSP) linked into Wechat (another MSP) is another example. Complementary networks are very common in China, where much of the mobile world has collapsed to a few powerful ecosystems (Alibaba, Tencent, Baidu).

However, **inter-connected platforms** are arguably even better. This is when a platform (or set of features) is actually integrated within another platform - to the point that the whole thing becomes inseparable within a service. The feature the user group sees and uses is actually being delivered by several interconnected platforms. For example, advertising-based media (e.g., Yahoo, broadcast TV) is increasingly inter-connected with advertising networks (i.e,. platforms that match advertising buyers with available inventory in real-time). That's how the ads on Yahoo, Baidu and Google get placed in real-time based on who you are or what you are looking at. There are actually +2 interconnected MSPs delivering this service.

* * *

Ok, that was quite a bit theory. But I think it was necessary to explain how these types of platforms compete. I will cite a lot of this in the following article. Now onto what Airbnb should do different than Uber in China.

WHAT AIRBNB SHOULD DO DIFFERENTLY THAN UBER IN CHINA

By Jeffrey Towson

In the previous article, I laid out some basic theory for how platform businesses compete. Based on this thinking, I think Airbnb should do 6 things differently than Uber in China.:

#1: AIRBNB WILL NEED TO CRACK THE CODE FOR CHINESE HOME-SHARING.

Unlike in ride-sharing and taxi-hailing, the right services and pricing for home-sharing in China are still unclear. This is the biggest difference between Uber and Airbnb's situation in China.

When Uber entered China in late 2014, Kuaidi and Didi already had riders in hundreds of cities (mostly through taxi hailing). Didi and Kuaidi had mostly solved the services, features, and "chicken-and-egg" problems. Pricing still wasn't clear as they were using venture capital money to subsidize drivers, build critical mass and kill off competitors. By the time Uber entered, it was mostly a question of who was going to get to scale first – and achieve a network effect and economies of scale. The services provided were pretty clear.

However, in Chinese home-sharing, this question is still unclear. Market leaders Tujia and Xiaozhu have not gotten big adoption (450,000 listings and 100,000 listings). They have struggled both to get quality listings on their platforms and to convince travelers to stay in other people's homes. In particular, they have struggled with a big lack of trust in the market. Also, keep in mind, hotels in China are quite cheap, which is a big difference with home-sharing in the West. Short-term rentals, especially in vacation spots, are also a big established business in China, albeit run in a B2C manner.

As a result, the business models seen today in Chinese home-sharing are pretty different. Xiaozhu is kind of like Airbnb (a C2C model), but they also offer renovation services to get quality home listings. Xiaozhu staff will actually go and decorate the home listings themselves. It is basically a C2C platform with lots of additional services.

In contrast, market leader Tujia is mostly a B2C model and much more like a short-term home rental service. They work with property developers and many of their listings are properties within holiday resorts, often owned by asset management companies. They also directly control their core listings. On the traveler-side, they are more focused more on vacation rentals and holiday housing for families. There are actually a lot of standardization and quality benefits with this type of B2C approach.

Basically, nobody has cracked the code for Chinese home-sharing yet. And as mentioned in Part 1, this is fairly common in two-sided networks. It is often the 3rd or 4th entrant that gets it right, not the first mover. And if they do figure it out, they still need to get around the chicken-and-egg problem.

Airbnb is arriving in a still nascent home-sharing market in China. This is good for them and a much better situation than Uber faced, basically playing catch-up to Kuaidi-Didi. Airbnb will need to crack this code ASAP. And they may need to drastically change their business model to do so. The quality and independence of their China management is going to be a critical issue.

#2: AIRBNB SHOULD FOCUS FIRST ON DOMINATING CHINA'S OUTBOUND HOME-SHARING MARKET.

In 2015, over 110M Chinese tourists flew overseas – where they stayed in hotels, short-term rentals and / or home-shares. Note: over 50% of tourists in Asia this past year were from China.

This part of the market is much clearer. First, one side of the platform (the listed homes) is already in place. Second, the price differential for home shares versus hotels in places like New York and London is much more compelling. Especially for families. And third, the chicken-and-egg problem is already solved. The international platform is up and running.

Uber did not have this type of cross-border market in China. Airbnb does and should try to dominate it quickly.

Airbnb's first line of attack can be a horizontal attack on travel agencies (an MSP vs. VI attack). They can use their big MSP to subsidize the prices to Chinese tourists currently using travel agencies and packages. Chinese tourists do not really travel independently yet. They prefer flight and hotel packages (plus visa and other services). Organized tour groups are also popular.

However, two MSP competitors are operating in this space, Ctrip and Zhubaijia. Zhubaijia offers all-in-one outbound services, including accommodations, car rentals and customized guided tours for Chinese travelers. They are bundling home-sharing with other services. And they are providing quality control for Chinese families on their trips, such as convenient locations, quality checks, security, etc. However, Ctrip is the big competitor and will discussed in the next section.

Uber never had this type of cross-border market when it entered China. The ride-sharing market is mostly locally. I would argue it is mostly city-by-city. Adding drivers in Chengdu doesn't really benefit riders much in Beijing. But home-sharing is a naturally international market. So Airbnb should focus on this outbound segment. The market is big and clear – and they have strong advantages already in place.

#3: AIRBNB SHOULD WORRY ABOUT CTRIP. THIS IS THEIR BIGGEST THREAT.

In September, Airbnb announced it has had "a 500% increase in outbound travel from China in just the past year." They also said "since 2008, there [has] been over 2 million guest arrivals from China at Airbnb listings worldwide." These numbers strike me as pretty suspect (if you have good numbers in 2016, you don't point all the way back to 2008). But let's assume they have some decent adoption in China today.

As mentioned, there is no chicken-and-egg problem for Airbnb cross-border. They already have an international network of apartments and guests. And, most importantly, they already have many of the strengths I mentioned in Part 1: a network effect, economies of scale in operations and marketing, a full suite of features and services, an ability to bundle services, and an ability to subsidize across their MSP.

I don't think Chinese competitors can compete with them internationally in home-sharing. It is very difficult to launch an international two-sided network in general. But to do so against an entrenched incumbent is next to impossible. So I think Tujia and Xiaozhu on their own have very little chance against Airbnb outside of China. However, Ctrip is a serious competitor internationally. They are making moves in this area (i.e., their recent acquisition of UK-based Skyscanner). They also are the largest investor in Tujia.

Ctrip should worry Airbnb. My next article on the US-China platform wars is about Ctrip vs. Expedia internationally. I will discuss this more there.

#4: AIRBNB SHOULD TRY TO MARRY ALIBABA OR TENCENT - PREFERABLY BOTH.

When Uber entered China, Kuaidi and Didi were already partnered with Alibaba and Tencent. Their ride-sharing services were integrated, to some degree, into these big ecosystems. As mentioned in Part 1, complementary and inter-linked MSPs can be a big advantage. Uber, in contrast, was not even available on Wechat at certain times. It is worth remembering that the BATs carry over 50% of all the mobile data traffic for China. Being on these big platforms matters.

However, Tencent and Alibaba are still unattached when it comes to home-sharing (mostly). Tujia has backing from Ctrip (and therefore Baidu, sort of). But Alibaba and Tencent are the bigger platforms and are mostly unaligned.

Airbnb should partner with Alibaba and / or Tencent today. Lock one or both of them up. Integrate your service with their ecosystems as much as possible. This is a very big deal. And as Airbnb China is now a separate business, they could sell part of that to Alibaba or Tencent.

#5: AIRBNB SHOULD SUBSIDIZE CHINESE TRAVELERS AND START A MONEY WAR.

Airbnb already has two big groups of users internationally (listings and travelers). Currently, Tujia doesn't really have scale in either group (in terms of revenue). So Airbnb should subsidize prices to Chinese home-owners and travelers. Offer prices that will encourage usage and that Tujia and Xiaozhu simply can't match.

This approach can be amplified with raised capital. Airbnb has a big fundraising advantage over Tujia and Xiaozhu. At a +$30B valuation, it can raise $1-2b with little dilution. The local players probably cannot match this.

Basically, Airbnb China should start a money war - and use subsidies to both drive adoption and kill competitors. But this does depend on figuring out the pricing and services equation first.

Recall, much of the Uber vs. Didi fight was really a money war. It was about who could outspend the other in driver and rider subsidies. And as neither could outspend the other, they eventually sued for peace. However, Airbnb can outspend its current China rivals and it should. However, Ctrip will be a problem in this regard.

#6: AIRBNB SHOULD "BE LIKE TRAVIS" IN ATTITUDE.

Finally, Airbnb should copy the attitude of Uber CEO Travis Kalanick in China. Chinese companies will often bleed the foreigner in terms of cash to see if they will give up and go home. It's a common tactic. To his credit, Travis made it clear he was coming to China to win. He spent $2B fighting Didi. He showed total commitment. And very quickly, everyone gave up on the idea of scaring him off. Note: He would never had walked away with 18% of Didi if there was any doubt about his willingness to keep fighting.

Airbnb will need to show this same "burn the boats behind us" total dedication to China.

So far, the Airbnb team in China has not done this. They have been cautious in their statements but they look pretty good overall. Their new China head is a China veteran. They have the right backers (Sequoia Capital, China Broadband Capital). They have said they are staffing up to +300 people in China (still only 10% of Tujia's staffing). Overall, things look good so far. But I argue they will eventually need to write big checks and show a Travis-like attitude.

If they do this, then there are probably two outcomes for them. They will win the market or they end up with significant minority stake in the China winner (like Uber did). Both are great outcomes. Keep in mind, Uber's stake in Didi is already worth $7B. And will could be worth a lot more than that one day.

Two More Asides

Time for another breather. Here are a couple of light articles on being a pretty introverted person in the international business world.

STOP CALLING ME AN INTROVERT. I PREFER "POWER THINKER"

By Jeffrey Towson

I'm really getting sick of the term "introvert". It sounds like someone with a problem. Like someone who is anti-social. In contrast, "extrovert" sounds outgoing and engaging. Like the CEO or student body president.

Yes, I admit some of us are pretty quiet in classrooms, at dinner parties and during corporate functions. Yes, we do find parties tiring after an hour or two. And yes, we usually let the phone ring through to voicemail (it's distracting).

But none of this is because we are anti-social. In fact, one-on-one we are pretty chatty. It's mostly because noise and crowds are overstimulating and prevent us from doing what we do best, which is deep thinking.

Most introverts I know are basically full-time thinkers. They are thinking about something all the time. And I assert that we do deep thinking better than other people. That will sound arrogant to the extroverts, who will say "Well, we can do deep thinking too". My answer is "No, you can't. Not like us."

The difference, as I see it is, is this:

- Extroverts like to go to conferences, parties and corporate retreats. They enjoy them and get charged up by the interactions. However, introverts get exhausted by the noise and people. We know what the term "people exhaustion" means. So naturally, extroverts are better at people-based activities, like leading big organizations and sales.

- However, introverts get similarly charged up when we can find a quiet place to focus on a problem. Put an extrovert alone in an office for three days and he/she will get tired and lonely. In contrast, we will get charged up and increasingly focused. So naturally, we're better at thinking-based activities, like research and writing.

So can we lose the term "introvert"?. How did we get labeled by the negative side of our habits anyways? Extroverts aren't routinely called "annoying over-talkers". From now on, I'm going with "power thinker". That's a better description.

"Extrovert" and "power thinker" are both good terms. They are both positive and aspirational - something one can strive to be in life. The extroverts can aspire to become Jack Welch and Steve Jobs. We power thinkers can look up to Warren Buffett and Bill Gates. Certainly, nobody has ever dreamed of becoming an introvert.

That's a bit of ranting and generalizing. Here are some examples from my own life:

- I have a friend Amy who is an uber-extrovert. She is unbelievable. She probably meets 20-30 new people per day. In the office. At meetings. On the street. In Starbucks. I have watched her go into a cocktail meet-and-greet and know everyone in about an hour. And not just hellos and handing business cards. She will get to know them and keep in touch. It's amazing to watch, like I am observing some other species than myself.

- However, I notice I am similarly extreme in things that she probably views as bizarre. For example, I will often get working on a problem and then forget to eat. Not just a meal, but often for the whole day. And back in graduate school, I would frequently forget to eat for 2-3 days at a time (usually dropping from 140 to 120 lbs during finals). But, far from being tired or exhausted from this, I would become more and more charged up as the days went by. In fact, there was almost a euphoric feeling. So I'm sure Amy probably sees me as quite bizarre as well.

- Another example. I have one particularly brainy friend (hi Ranwa) who seems to balance being analytical with also being a great executive at a large (and famous) internet company. She seems to be an ambivert, able to operate in both ways. I find myself in awe of her ability to do this but I also cringe at the thought of having to be in such a corporate environment myself. The term "team building exercise" literally makes me shudder.

- But again, I think I also have habits that would make such an ambivert cringe. For example, I find myself looking forward to taking 2 week trips for thinking and writing books. I rent a beach house and then write 12-14 hours per day. And I will feel more and more energetic as the week goes on. I also find my thinking gets better and better. I suspect my ambivert friend would hate the idea of doing something like this.

Anyways, I'm going with "power thinker" from now on. It's positive and a bit cocky (kind of like extrovert).

Looking back at my life, it seems logical to me that some people are just more hard-wired for contemplation. All I've ever really wanted to do with my life is sit in a bar and do math problems. But nobody (yet) has been willing to pay me to do this. If you know of someone, please send them my way.

MY PLAYBOOK FOR SUCCESS AS AN INTROVERT

By Jeffrey Towson

Recently, I argued that the term "introvert" should be replaced with "power thinker". My follow-up to that article is the following simple playbook for having an impact as an introvert (i.e., as a power thinker).

My playbook is just three points.

POINT 1: FOCUS ON ONE QUESTION THAT WILL MAKE ALL THE DIFFERENCE.

If your strength is thinking, then you want to focus on 1-2 really important questions. You don't want to move around. You don't want to answer questions that others can answer. You want to pick 1-2 really important questions and then keep going deeper and deeper into them. And you keep at it until you're the best person on that topic.

This could be called the Albert Einstein rule. When asked to explain his success in life, he said "If I had an hour to solve a problem and my life depended on the solution, I would spend the first 55 minutes determining the proper question to ask, for once I know the proper question, I could solve the problem in less than five minutes."

I personally prefer the advice of Carlyle co-founder David Rubenstein. He basically said you should never study anything that doesn't make you money.

Either way, the point is the same. Focus on 1-2 questions. And make sure they are the ones that will make all the difference in your business and life. For me, that means:

- A question that will make me money.

-It is something I think I can do better than others. For example, I don't do real estate. It's interesting but everyone seems pretty good at it.

- It is something I am fascinated by.

In my business / life, I eventually settled on the question: **Does this company have a durable competitive advantage?** And I spend most of my time trying to answer it in quirky markets and complicated situations. I want to know which company is going to do well before it is clear to others. Plus a competitive advantage also often makes it easier to do a solid valuation.

In more technical terms, I focus on "competitive advantage in special situations". This could be multinationals struggling in China, companies operating in highly political markets (like healthcare and State capitalism), young companies just emerging, advantages that are unique to developing economies, advantages from software and other new digital processes, and so on.

POINT 2: TRACK THE 2-3 OUTCOMES THAT MATTER MOST.

If I spend 80% of my time thinking about the above one question, how do I translate that into a valuable outcome? For me, the two outcomes I track are:

- Investment returns (i.e,. turning analysis / thinking into wealth). If you can identify which company is going to do well before others in various situations, you know what to buy. Note: I also find this particular expertise can lead to lots of advisory work.

- Talks and keynote speeches. If I am making progress against an important question, I find that speaking invitations tend to follow. This is also a good way to meet people who are interested in the same question.

POINT 3: HAVE TOOLS THAT CONVERT YOUR THINKING INTO YOUR DESIRED OUTCOMES.

I am looking for the shortest distance between my thinking (Point 1) and the outcomes I want (Point 2). And as a professional thinker, I want minimal execution. Not too many meetings. No operations.

No building of anything. I want to spend 80% of my time thinking - and then the two outcomes to follow almost immediately from this.

For me the biggest tool for this is an investment team and/or platform. Lots of systematic thinking, levered up by a team and then a purchase. Warren Buffett is the model and he is arguably the world's most effective and efficient introvert. His 23 person company in Omaha is now worth over $400B.

But you can really point to lots of companies in finance, Hollywood and technology that are effective at this sort of direct translation between thinking and outcome. Software, in particular, seems to directly translate thinking into profitable companies and widely-used technology.

A second tool I use are daily habits. I follow a routine that keeps most of my day focused on thinking (i.e., no phones, no internet, no meetings, etc.). Every day, I make sure I do my 4-5 key habits. These are cumulative habits that add up over time and move me forward.

In general, I'm a big believer in doing the same activities day after day. It's a good way to get cumulative results over time. And you get more efficient and effective when you do the same things over and over.

Finally, I consider writing and teaching as tools in my playbook. I write one article per week and one book per year. I find good writing requires good thinking. I like the phrase "if you didn't write it you don't know it." I also use the writing process to figure out business questions I don't understand (I keep a list of these questions on my iPad).

*   *   *

Anyways, that is my introvert playbook. Focus on 1-2 questions that will make a difference. Track the outcomes. And build tools to achieve them that are cumulative over time if you just stick at it.

*   *   *

Ok. Now back to our final contrarian point about China.

SECTION IV
AT HOME AND ABROAD, CHINESE COMPANIES CAN BEAT YOU FAIR AND SQUARE

Chinese companies have gotten to global scale in record time. They are now global in the sense that they have scale, they are competing with global players in and beyond China and they are at global levels of capability. According to a recent analysis by MGI, the top quartile of Chinese companies now earn returns comparable to US companies. And among the top 5,000 companies worldwide by market capitalization (2015), Chinese (excluding Hong Kong) companies now account for 1,107, a significant rise from 326 back in 2000.

Most of this is because these companies are big in China. China now has 110 companies in the Fortune 500, even though less than 15% of their revenues come from outside China. One implication of this is they have a lot of global growth potential provided they are competitive. And that is the point of this section .The best Chinese players can now compete with companies virtually anywhere – and they can win fair and square. Companies like Huawei, ZTE,

Midea, Lenovo, and Chinachem are already dominating their industries globally.

Much of this competitive ability globally is because competition in the Mainland remains brutal. Competitors rise and fall quickly, depending on the industry. The levels of technology and other capabilities advance very rapidly. Jeff has frequently described competition in China as the world's most well-capitalized knife fight – and something that is routinely underestimated.

It is the winners of these brutal domestic markets that are now going global. When you look at someone like Alibaba's Jack Ma, try to imagine how many thousands of competitors (including eBay) he has beaten over the past twenty years. Chinese CEOs are the Spartans of global business. And they are coming to your market right now.

In this final section, we present nine essays on the brutal but entertaining competitive fights happening in modern China – and increasingly internationally.

FAILURE ISN'T FINAL IN CHINA (I): DANONE AND CARLSBERG BEER

By Jeffrey Towson

The Chinese market is difficult and failure is common. This is true for both domestic and foreign companies. But the country is also huge and there is almost always another opportunity available. The brutality of the Chinese market is compensated for by its breadth.

French food company Danone and Danish brewer Carlsberg Group provide good examples of what to do when you struggle in China. Both were confronted with serious problems. And their responses hold important lessons. One went on to a reasonable outcome, and the other to great success.

Danone's biggest move into China was a 51/49 joint venture with Hangzhou Wahaha Group, formed in 1996. It was a fairly typical inbound development deal based on combining foreign expertise, products and capital with local management and distribution, especially into secondary cities.

The joint venture grew rapidly and expanded from a small struggling beverage company into a conglomerate of over 40 food joint ventures in milk drinks, soft drinks, bottled water, teas and fruit juices. Over the course of 10 years, Danone and Wahaha built the largest beverage company in China.

The joint venture, however, made headlines in 2007 -- after a dispute between the parties erupted. This led to legal action in both Hangzhou and Los Angeles. There was a lot of sniping in the press. Eventually, Danone sold its stake in the joint venture to Wahaha in 2009.

Carlsberg's problems in China did not get this type of press. They happened fairly quietly.

The brewer arrived in 1981, at first limiting itself to importing beer and operating a Hong Kong brewery. It made its first major move on the mainland in 1995 with the acquisition of a brewery in Huizhou, Guangdong Province. This would become the company's main hub in China. It also invested in a Shanghai brewery and began producing there in 1998. Unlike Danone, it did not really form a partnership on the mainland.

But like most international brewers, Carlsberg struggled in China. Small state-owned breweries already existed in almost every Chinese city. This legacy meant there was already a lot of beer infrastructure and that Chinese consumers were accustomed to very low-priced beer.

Later, foreign entrants had to contend with these small state-owned breweries being rolled up into state-owned giants. By the late 1990s, China was still an unprofitable beer market – and large shares of it were held by state-owned Tsingtao Brewery, Beijing Yanjing Brewery and China Resources Snow Breweries.

In 1999, Carlsberg effectively gave up on China. It sold its Shanghai brewery and let its staff go. Sunny Wong, one of its key China sales people, left the country and returned to the U.K. More on him in a moment.

Danone left with a bang. Carlsberg left quietly. What happened to both after, though, is important.

In 2002-2003, Carlsberg suddenly reappeared in China. It is not clear who made the decision or why. But it relaunched its China operations and took everyone by surprise with its strategy: It basically ignored the major cities and beer markets of Shanghai, Beijing and the east coast. Instead, it went far west, into China's big backyard.

These western regions, including the provinces of Gansu, Qinghai, Xinjiang and Yunnan, remain relatively undeveloped today. Back in 2003, they formed a vast nowhere, by far the poorest part of China. There was little infrastructure and even less money.

Around 2002, Sunny Wong had returned from the U.K. with what he would later describe as his "mission impossible" -- to develop

Carlsberg's western China business in places he had never been before. He promptly flew to Yunnan and Tibet, and over the next couple years put together a flurry of joint ventures and development deals across the region.

By 2006, Carlsberg had over 20 breweries in western China. It also had become the market leader in all the western provinces in which it had invested. Its network would eventually expand to more than 39 breweries in central and western China. Today, Carlsberg has more than a 60% share of the market in western China, where beer consumption is growing at a 12% annual clip, compared with 4% to 5% nationally.

Carlsberg has also expanded into Chongqing, in central China. For most companies, starting operations in Chongqing is considered moving inland. For Carlsberg, it was actually a move toward the east. In Yunnan, the company is building what will be its second largest brewery anywhere in the world.

The story for Danone has been quite different. Following their exit from the Wahaha deal, they met with multiple other potential partners. And following China's 2008 powdered milk contamination scandals, Danone found itself well-positioned in the infant nutrition market in China. Food scandals and a general lack of trust in domestic brands have led to a massive increase in imports of foreign milk formula. More than 30% of baby formula is now purchased online, and it is common for vacationing Chinese to bring home suitcases full of powdered milk.

Danone and other foreign leaders like Mead Johnson and Nestle are now well-positioned in China. Things are starting to look better and better for Danone in China.The lesson being with 1.4 billion consumers, there is always another opportunity in China.

I think there are three important lessons in these stories:

1. Things change very fast in China. So there are always new opportunities. However, bear in mind that this works both ways. Success in China is also not necessarily forever.

2. If you are partnering with local companies, you need something of value to add long-term. Think brands, technology, foreign customers and foreign products. And be conscious of when they are no longer going to be of as much value. Get a prenuptial agreement (to use the marriage metaphor).

3. When going directly into China without a local partner, the key question is how to avoid or beat the competition. You need a powerful answer to this question. It is far better and cheaper to avoid this struggle altogether, if you can. Carlsberg did this by going west. Danone is doing this now by focusing on infant nutrition.

Re-printed with permission of Nikkei Asian Review (link here)

In this final section, we present nine essays on the brutal but entertaining competitive fights happening within modern China – and increasingly internationally.

FAILURE ISN'T FINAL IN CHINA (II): FORD AND FIAT

By Jeffrey Towson

In Part 1, I wrote about how both Carlsberg and Danone encountered setbacks in China. And then how Carlsberg,in particular, came back and succeeded.

In this article, I have two more examples of "what to do when things go wrong in China". This time in automotive. I think the story of Ford in China is pretty inspiring. But first Fiat, which is a fairly short story.

NANJING FIAT: STRUGGLE TO LAUNCH IN THE PRC

Italian automaker Fiat entered China in 1996 through a 50/50 joint venture with Nanjing Auto. As foreign auto companies can only operate with a local partner, there was a lot of jockeying for dance partners in the 1980s and 90s. GM partnered with SAIC (really the Shanghai government). Volkswagen partnered with both SAIC and FAW. Fiat partnered with Nanjing Auto.

Nanjing Auto is reported to be the oldest of the Chinese automobile manufacturers (although FAW was the first to actually make cars). Nanjing Auto was originally an auto workshop. But in the late 1940's, the army began working with it as they passed through Nanjing and began using it for repairs. The company was later transferred to a ministry. And it eventually began making trucks in 1958.

Nanjing Auto's joint venture with Fiat was a fairly standard deal based on combining foreign capital and technology with local operating and government expertise (important in cars in China).

Over the next six years, the JV produced only four models (the Perla, the Siena, the Palio compact and the Palio Weekend station wagon). This is a very low number in this fast-moving market. Sales averaged 25,000-35,000 annually from 2002 to 2006. In comparison, SAIC-GM sold 413,000 cars in 2006 alone.

The joint venture basically never really got launched. This was mostly the result of having the wrong partner. Nanjing Auto was primarily a truck-maker and the Nanjing city government could only offer limited support. In contrast, Shanghai supplied GM and Volkswagen with extensive support, including building an entire auto supply chain and making large government car and taxi fleet purchases.

The JV ended in 2007 and Fiat exited. Nanjing Auto later became part of SAIC.

CHANGAN FORD: LATE TO THE CHINA MARKET

Ford entered China through a similar joint venture with Changan Auto in 2001. They were pretty late coming to China and then things happened a bit slowly. They began by assembling Ford Fiestas from kits.

Mazda also entered the picture. In 2005, they bought 15% of the Changan Ford joint venture, which was renamed the Changan Ford Mazda Automobile Co. And production became focused in Chongqing and Nanjing. There were also lots of announcements about big investments and capacity building.

But for all this building and deal structuring, the car sales didn't really happen. By 2006, the JV was selling about 126,000 cars per year. More than Fiat, but only a third of GM and Volkswagen.

Post Break-Up, Changan Ford Comes Roaring Back

However,in recent years, things have really started to change for Ford. They have split from Mazda and their recent performance is starting to turn heads.

In December 2012, the Chinese government approved the split up of the three-way joint venture between Ford, Mazda and Changan Automobile. The now renamed Changan Ford joint venture went on to sell an **impressive 678,000 cars in China** in 2013. And that was a 49% increase year-over-year. And it was up from only around 300,000 for the JV as recently as 2010.

By 2014, according to the China Association of Automobile Manufacturers, the Changan Ford Focus was number one in China with 391,781 units sold. And this was the third time in a row that the Focus has claimed the top sales position.

The company is still behind leaders GM and Volkswagen overall but they are coming up fast. For several years, Ford grew at 3x the industry average. And in 2014, they were 8th in China for car sales. As we are going to print, Ford just broke 1M in sales for 2016 in China (joint venture plus Ford sales combined).

Fiat Is Coming Back to China

In 2010, Fiat found a new China partner, Guangzhou Automobile Group Co. (GAC). Sales began in September 2012. Also, Fiat became Fiat Chrysler along the way. In 2013, they reportedly sold approximately 130,000 cars in China.

I think there are some important lessons here.

LESSON 1: YOU DON'T NECESSARILY NEED TO GET TO CHINA EARLY TO WIN.

Ford only really started producing cars in China in significant numbers in 2005 (61,000 sold in 2005). This was way behind General Motors, which established its joint venture with SAIC in 1997. And it was decades after Volkswagen launched its China joint venture in 1984.

Being early is an advantage for sure. But in some businesses, it is never too late go after the China market.

LESSON 2: YOU DON'T NEED TO START OFF IN FIRST TIER CITIES.

Ford did not partner with a major automotive group in a coastal first tier city. It did not go to Beijing, Shanghai or Shenzhen / Guangzhou. It went to Chongqing, far inland.

While I have not seen Ford's sales breakdown by region, it would not be surprising to see the company doing particularly well in the inland markets. Like Carlsberg, going deeper inland and perhaps avoiding the more entrenched competition in the coastal cities, was a good strategy.

The other factor here is that an inland headquarters has the advantage of lower labor costs. Manufacturers are increasingly moving inland to avoid rising labor costs on the coast.

LESSON 3: MARKET SHARE CAN SHIFT FAIRLY QUICKLY IN CHINA

General Motors' auto sales increased to about 3.9 million in China in 2016. That is up from 3.6 million in 2015. Volkswagen is in the same sales range. There is definitely some market stability at the front of the pack.

However, market share in the middle shifts quickly. In the past years, Ford has surpassed Toyota and its two joint-venture partners which sold 917,500 cars (a 9% increase). Ford also passed Honda's China volume at 756,000 cars (a 26% increase). So market share can move quickly in the middle.

LESSON 4: IT'S MOSTLY ABOUT GETTING TO LOCAL OPERATING SCALE

Ford has been investing in China in a big way. With $4.9 billion in investment set for China, Ford and its joint venture partners are building four assembly plants and three powertrain plants. It has also announced plans to double its network of 400 dealers and is launching 15 vehicles in the next several years.

The lesson here is that local operational scale is the key capability to watch over time. Long-term that is how you win in China. And all indications are that Ford is continuing to aggressively build scale on the ground in China.

FAILURE ISN'T FINAL IN CHINA (III): MORGAN STANLEY AND EXPEDIA.

By Jeffrey Towson

This is the third in a series of articles on companies that have had difficulties in China. However, in many cases, they later came back and won, often spectacularly.

In Part 1, I detailed how Carlsberg beer and Danone both initially struggled in China. But Carlsberg later came back with an impressive success in the far West. In Part 2, I detailed how Ford and Fiat both encountered challenges in China. But in the past several years, Ford has been showing impressive sales across China.

In this article, I look at Morgan Stanley and Expedia. I find Morgan Stanley's China story pretty inspiring. But first Expedia, which is more complicated.

EXPEDIA IN CHINA

Expedia entered China in 2005 with the purchase of a 55% controlling stake in Chinese travel site eLong. And Expedia basically did everything right - including:

- They positioned themselves against big China trends: rising consumers, surging travel (both domestic and international) and e-commerce.

- They got to the market early and had a first mover advantage. Back in 2005, the Chinese Internet was still in its infancy. And this was also +5 years before Chinese consumers would really start traveling and spending.

- They got to scale in a business with strong network economics. The online marketplace for hotels (not plane flights) quickly collapsed to a handful of dominant giants. And Expedia, via eLong, was one of these big winners. Qunar and ctrip were the others.

- In 2011, they purchased an additional 8% of eLong from Renren for $72M. This took them to 62% ownership.

It all looked pretty good. So why in 2015 did they sell their entire eLong stake for $671M?

My assessment is that they got tired of losing money. The online travel market of China is ferociously competitive. eLong was frequently losing money and impacting Expedia's overall returns.

In the most recent quarters before Expedia's exit, eLong was still periodically losing around $20M per quarter.

This is an example of "last man standing". Competitors in China will often ramp up spending on capacity and price subsidies - and everyone begins losing money. The market then becomes a contest of who is willing and able to lose the most cash. In the end, whoever is "left standing" gets the market. Uber China and DidiChuxing recently had this same situation.

So Expedia won big in China and became one of the three major players. But they were still losing cash after ten years of work. And it appears they eventually had enough. They sold their stake in eLong, much of which was then purchased by ctrip.Ctrip is now expected to show a significant margin expansion.

MORGAN STANLEY AND CICC

CICC (China International Capital Corp) was launched in 1995 as a joint venture between Morgan Stanley and China Construction Bank (i.e., People's Construction Bank of China). For Morgan Stanley, this was their single largest investment in an emerging market to date ($35M for 34.3% ownership). And it was their primary strategy for becoming a player in China's domestic capital market.

The joint venture was very successful. CICC has gone from the 40 employees at launch to over 4,200 employees today. Revenues in 2015 were over 9B RMB.

However, Morgan Stanley sold its stake in CICC in 2011 - and had been trying to sell as early as 2008. There are various reasons for this, including the financial crisis and dealing with limits on how many banks / JVs a foreign company can have in this sector in China. But underneath this was also the fact that CICC was no longer an operational vehicle for Morgan Stanley in China. It had become mostly a passive investment.

So what happened?

My standard question for any company in China is "what is your advantage or value-add to your partner?". Good answers to this can be technology, foreign customers, a well-known brand, and cross-border operations. But my follow-up question is always "and how long will this advantage or value add last?". This is the question that usually catches companies.

A lot of the joint venture stories you hear are after one partner's capital, expertise or technology has already been transferred. A declining value-add by a partner (on either side) can easily lead a break-up or to one party getting pushed aside. Your ongoing value-add is what really keeps you in the relationship.

For Morgan Stanley and CICC, this happened quite quickly. The first group of investment bankers were trained. The importance of foreign capital declined. Morgan Stanley had added a lot of initial value but then more or less stopped having a significant operational role and became more of a passive shareholder.

This type of result would have been fine if they were a venture capital firm (they made a very good return on their $35M). But this was not their primary goal as an MNC looking at the China market long-term.

POST BREAK-UP, MORGAN STANLEY KEEPS ROLLING.

However, this situation did not really slow Morgan Stanley down. Investment bankers are pretty clever.

- In 2006, Morgan Stanley became the first foreign bank to receive a wholly-owned commercial banking license in China.

- In 2008, they created a trust joint venture, Hangzhou Industrial and Commercial Trust. They also partnered with Huaxin Securities to form a fund management company, Morgan Stanley Huaxin Fund Management Company.

- In 2011, they established a RMB private equity investment management firm.They also partnered with Huaxin Securities to create Morgan Stanley Huaxin Securities.

And all of this was done under some fairly strict limits on what foreign banks can do in China.

* * *

The bad news is, yes, China is a difficult and often brutal market. Struggle is, in fact, very common. The good news is that the market is so big and dynamic that you can almost always try again. So keep trying. Don't give up. But wear a cup.

THE BATTLE BETWEEN UBER AND DIDI CHUXING CONTINUES – BUT IN SE ASIA

By Jeffrey Towson

In August 2016, DidiChuxing bought Uber China. This was the end of a long and expensive fight for the Chinese ride-sharing market. With their merger, they officially became friends. But only in China. And definitely not in Southeast Asia.

Following the sale of its China business to Didi last week, Uber began immediately refocusing on other regions, with Southeast Asia appearing high on their list. In response, Didi (and Japanese Softbank) almost immediately announced a new fundraising round for their local SE Asia ride-sharing ally Grab.

So Round 2 of the Uber vs. Didi fight started almost immediately. It is in Southeast Asia - and who might acquire Grab just became an interesting question.

My take on this is four points.

POINT 1: THE VIEW FROM BEIJING IS AWESOME.

Beijing-based Didi now has +95% market share in Chinese ride-sharing, although this depends on how you define the market. China is already the world's largest on-demand transportation market by far. By ride volume, it is larger than the US, Europe, India and all the rest of the world combined. Of the over 6B trips projected for 2017, Didi will, in theory, have +4B of them. That is amazing.

Didi no longer has any serious domestic competitors. They are sitting on +$10B in cash. Basically, their view from Beijing is awesome. Although changing regulations in China will be an ongoing issue.

Southeast Asia is now an interesting question for Didi. This is not some far-away international market they may or may not want. Chinese businesses are rapidly expanding across Asia. Tens of millions of their customers are already traveling to SE Asia every year. They need to decide if they want or need the SE Asian market. And what if Uber or another foreign competitor captures it instead?

POINT 2: SOUTHEAST ASIA IS STILL AN OPPORTUNITY - BUT NOT FOR LONG.

Uber is already present in most of SE Asia (Singapore, Thailand, Vietnam, Malaysia, Indonesia, Philippines and others). But they are really only in about 15 cities and they entered most of these in just the past 2-3 years. They are certainly not dominant yet.

Local competitor and Didi-investee Grab (formerly GrabTaxi) has a longer history in the region, having launched in Malaysia in 2012. They are mainly in six countries (Malaysia, Philippines, Thailand, Singapore, Vietnam, Indonesia) and claim 350,000 drivers, 19 million app downloads, +50% of private rides and +90% of taxi-hailing.

But they are also not dominant in the region yet. They are still in only about 30 cities in total and they are by far the smallest of the five main on demand transportation companies globally (Uber, Lyft, Didi, Ola, GrabTaxi). Their latest funding round likely values them at $3B, a fraction of Uber's $66B, Didi's $33B, and even Ola's $5B.

Go-Jek is an interesting new competitor, focusing on motorcycles and rocketing upwards this past year. They remain focused on Indonesia (+250M people) and they claim 200,000 motorbike drivers and several hundred thousand booking requests daily. And they have raised $550M at $1.3B valuation.

Overall, the SE Asia market is still a relatively open market with no dominant player. So if Didi wants to win in SE Asia, there is a window of opportunity.

POINT 3: DIDI CAN FOLLOW CHINESE CONSUMERS AND COMPANIES INTO SOUTHEAST ASIA.

Didi has serious advantages in Southeast Asia that should worry both Uber and Grab.

First, SE Asia receives tons of Chinese tourists. Chinese are the single largest tourist group in the Asia Pacific with over 50M visitors per year. Thailand expects about 10M Chinese tourists per year. Indonesia will likely receive +2M. And Chinese tourists are also among the world's top spending tourists per capita (average $875 each when traveling).

Second, Chinese companies are naturally expanding into SE Asia. China is going global and Asia is the first port of call. You can hear Mandarin and see Chinese signs across SE Asia now. And this is only a fraction of what it will be in 5-10 years.

Third, most of these Chinese tourists and business people already have Didi on their phones. They all definitely have WeChat, a Didi investor with +840M Chinese users. And they are increasingly using Alipay as they travel, another Didi investor with +450M Chinese users.

So Didi already has a big and growing customer base in SE Asia. Didi is now integral to Chinese businesses and the Baidu-Alibaba-Tencent ecosystem, both of which are also rapidly extending into the region.

POINT 4: DIDI COULD DOMINATE SOUTHEAST ASIA.

As we have seen in China, these fights can easily turn into "money wars", with competitors raising capital and then subsidizing drivers and customers. Grab doesn't have the capital to compete long-term with Uber or Didi in this way.

Another factor is the ferocity of "Team Didi". They won in China against strong local competitors. They went head-to-head with global giant Uber. And they have now assembled a team that consists of themselves, Tencent, Alibaba, Baidu and Apple. Team Didi plus $10B could dominate SE Asia if they wanted to.

* * *

I view SE Asia today as mostly a fight between Uber, Didi and Grab. And while Uber and Grab's plans are clear, Didi's is still unknown.

So let me pose a few final questions:

Does Didi really need SE Asia?

I think they do. Looking at how SE Asia will grow and integrate with China over the next 5-10 years, I think it a necessary ancillary market. Can Didi be the dominant on-demand transportation company of Asia without SE Asia?

If Didi doesn't fight for SE Asia, are they ok with Uber taking it?

Didi's operational tie-in and financial support for Grab may not be enough to stop Uber. If Didi isn't willing to enter the market directly, I think Uber taking the market is a real possibility.

Conversely, what if someone buys Grab? Uber?

The fight for Southeast Asia could turn into a fight to buy Grab. Didi is already a minority investor so I'm assuming they have some rights in any sales. But what if Uber or Didi were to buy Grab? Isn't that checkmate for SE Asia?

There are really lots of interesting questions in this situation. Here's my prediction: Didi will end up end buying Grab. But that's just a guess.

CHINESE BICYCLE-SHARING IS NOTHING LIKE RIDE-SHARING

By Jeffrey Towson

There has been a lot of talk about Chinese bicycle-sharing recently. In 2016, Tencent, Warburg Pincus and Sequoia participated in a $100M round for Shanghai-based Mobike. And Xiaomi, Citic PE and Coatue participated in a $130M round for Beijing-based Ofo. DidiChuxing is reported to have invested in Ofo as well.

Bike-sharing is now being proclaimed as a new frontier for Didi and for China's sharing economy (see articles here, here, here). But there's a problem.

- **Bike-sharing is not really sharing. It is not part of the sharing economy.**

- **Bike-sharing does not have a network effect.**
- **Bike-sharing has no real economies of scale (yet).**
- **There are some serious questions lingering about long-term consumer demand.**

Basically, bike-sharing is nothing like Didi, Grab, Ola, Uber, AirBnb and the others. Its economics are far more like an on-demand rental business or a vending machine business (at this point. It could evolve).

That doesn't mean it isn't a really great, scalable business. It well could be. And I hope it has explosive growth across China. I really like seeing Ofo's bright yellow bikes all over Peking University.

But much of the current excitement seems to be because people think this business is like Didi. It's just not. It's a different thing.

Here are four ways bike-sharing is different than ride-sharing.

1. BICYCLE-SHARING DOES NOT HAVE A NETWORK EFFECT.

Ride-sharing (i.e,. using cars) is awesome because it has a powerful competitive advantage via a two-sided network. Basically, each additional rider increases the networks' value to the drivers (i.e, more customers and they are closer by.). And each new driver increases the value of the service to each rider (i.e., shorter wait times, more cars available). So platforms with larger volumes actually have a superior service offering to both populations. And the market usually collapses to the leading companies quickly (Uber and Lyft in the USA, Didi in China, Ola in India, Grab in SE Asia, etc.).

Additionally, once the market has matured, it becomes very difficult for a new entrant to break in. If you then want to launch a ride-sharing service, you will have to offer the same large driver network and short wait times as the dominant competitors from day one. But to get all those drivers, you have to offer them a big customer base. It›s the multi-sided platform «chicken-and-egg» problem but with entrenched competitors. This type of indirect two-sided network effect also happens in home sharing (AirBnb), credit cards (Visa, MasterCard), app stores (Apple, Google Play), auction houses (Sotheby's, Christie's), and even shopping malls (sort of).

But none of this happens in bicycle-sharing. There is no second population of drivers using the platforms - and providing the cars (which are the key assets). You just need to put lots of bicycles around town. Each new rider does not add any value to the other riders, nor to a population of drivers.

Bike sharing is basically a traditional, vertically integrated b2c rental service. It is a traditional merchant business. Being bigger helps somewhat but it is still fairly easy for a new entrant to enter. All you would need is about 30,000 bicycles. That would cost about $2.5M. So this is a cheap and fairly easy business to enter, which will probably limit long-term profitability.

However, in the short-term companies like Ofo and Mobike should do really well. They are offering an innovative new service and are first-movers in a wide-open and massive market.

2. BICYCLE SHARING DOESN'T HAVE ECONOMIES OF SCALE (YET).

Another question is about the fixed costs and fixed assets, which can be another type of barrier to competition. If you have large fixed costs, a larger competitor can often provide a service cheaper on a per unit basis. Also, a big initial and / or ongoing capex requirement can deter entrants, such as in the constantly upgrading cable and telecommunications companies.

But neither fixed costs nor fixed assets appear to matter much in bike-sharing.The costs of placing and maintaining bicycles around the city doesn›t appear to be fixed or that big. It›s certainly not a significant deterrent to a well-funded, well-run competitor.

3. BIKE-SHARING IS NOT REALLY SHARING.

Ride-sharing is about gathering a population of drivers, who then provide and maintain their own cars. In AirBnb, people provide their homes. It's basically about using new digital technology to bring existing but unused supply into the market. It's a big deal.

For this type of platform, you don't have to own the assets or spend the capex to grow and maintain them. You can be the world's biggest car rental company without owning any cars. For the owners of these assets, they benefit from renting them out and dropping their effective cost. And for customers, they can cheaply utilize other people's assets - and theoretically avoid buying their own (in some cases).

But there isn't really any sharing happening in bike-sharing. Regardless of rider volume, the company must still buy and own all the bikes. And it must maintain them and replace them (say when they go missing). No assets are being shared.

So on the supply-side (over the long-term), this is a scalable service with no clear competitive advantages (yet). Again, think placing vending machines (and the Cokes) around town such that people can now buy Cokes whenever they pass by.

4. THERE ARE SOME INTERESTING QUESTIONS REGARDING CONSUMER DEMAND.

In the past +15 years, bike-sharing services have been launched in over 600 cities around the world. Most were local government initiatives. Some have been pretty successful. Many have failed, usually due to a lack of demand or bad management.

The real demand for as-needed bicycle trips "under three kilometers" is not totally clear yet. It could be limited, just a replacement for owning your own bike. Or it could induce lots of new and interesting uses. When you place bicycles within arms' reach of people at a negligible cost (1 RMB in China) people may start using them without thinking - and in lots of new ways. Vending machines didn't replace soda sales in supermarkets. People bought more because they passed the machines on the street and it cost basically nothing. The ability to leave the bike wherever you want is also a bit part of this.

One place we can see lots of cool new usage is with Ofo at Peking University. Those yellow bikes are literally everywhere. Another example are the bikes sitting outside of the subways. You get off the subway, pay 1 RMB, peddle the five blocks to your house and just drop the bike. That's pretty great. I think there are going to lots of surprises in how people start to use these bikes in Chinese cities.

However, my biggest concern for the customer proposition of bike-sharing is that it doesn't save you money. Home-sharing and car ride-sharing are convenient, like as-needed bicycles. But they can also be much cheaper than hotels (and sometimes taxis). And they are certainly cheaper than buying your own car or apartment. This kind of big cost saving doesn't happen with bike-sharing.

There are unfortunately lots of cheap ways to get around town in China. By metro, by taxi, by walking, by mototaxis, by scooters and by owning bicycles, many of which also cost next to nothing. And China is already over-run with bicycles, including mountain bikes, street bikes, fold-up bicycles, e-bikes and electric scooters. Note: new bicycles start at about 399 RMB at reputable stores.

So the consumer proposition for bike-sharing is mostly convenience plus negligible cost - not saving money.

Also keep in mind, riding a bicycle has some other issues. Like the weather, riding at night (no lights on these bikes), the requirement to peddle, and so on. Also, Beijing is cold and rainy in the winter. How many of these bikes are going to spend 3-4 months sitting unused in the snow and rain during the winter?

That said, there are tons of bicycles in China. You can see them on every street and in front of every building. So this is a bicycle country. Although increasingly what you see are scooters and e-bikes.

A FINAL POINT: THIS IS A REALLY NICE SERVICE. BUT I WOULD MARRY A BAT ASAP.

Most of what I just said you could also say about the iTunes store. Or about the super-popular beauty photo app Meitu. They are also mostly B2C services that operate as traditional merchants, not as multi-sided platforms. And these services also did really well in the short-term by being first movers with a cool new service.

But they eventually need to partner up with other services that have clearer business models and stronger competitive advantages (the iTunes store is mostly a merchant but the App Store is an MSP). And as Baidu, Alibaba and Tencent are +50% of all mobile internet usage in China, that's the target. Basically, bike-sharing should join Team Didi or Team Tencent ASAP and integrate their cool new service into a bigger ecosystem.

* * *

Overall, bike-sharing seems a really interesting new service. And they raise a neat question about what will people do with on-demand bicycles that are always within arms-reach at a negligible price? It is going to be fun to watch this play out in China's increasingly crowded cities.

THE RUTHLESS BUT ENTERTAINING FIGHT TO BECOME THE "FEDEX OF CHINA" (PART 1)

By Jeffrey Towson

SF Express, YTO, and the other China express delivery majors have been racing to go public. Faced with shrinking profits and mounting competitive threats, the dream of being the "Fedex of China" is quickly morphing into an arms race in capital and capabilities.

Here's my take on what is going on and what to expect. But first two quick background points.

BACKGROUND POINT 1: CHINESE EXPRESS DELIVERY IS AWESOME. THE MARKET IS HUGE, RAPIDLY GROWING, AND RIDING MULTIPLE CHINA TRENDS.

Chinese express delivery companies handled over 31 billion parcels in 2016. That was a greater volume than in the US and up from just 9 billion pieces in 2013. The volume is surging. It is projected to reach 20 billion parcels by 2020.

The revenues are also growing. Revenue in 2016 was 400B RMB, up from 30B RMB in 2006. YTO alone generated revenue of 25B RMB (2014).

It's just a huge and rapidly growing market. This is quite logical when you think of the China trends fueling this. Express delivery benefits from rising consumer spending, increasing retail activity, big industrial production, continued urbanization, inland development, still strong GDP growth and, of course, surging e-commerce. It's as good a macro story as you will see in China.

Within express delivery, private companies have been doing particularly well in the aggregate. In 2013, private Chinese courier companies accounted for two-thirds of the market by revenue and three-fourths by volume. For example, YTO delivered 2.1B packages in 2014 and has predicted growth of 50% per year through 2020.

So for all the talk about Alibaba, Tencent and the other Chinese Internet giants, the much-less-sexy express delivery business may be where the most predictable, long-term profits are.

BACKGROUND POINT 2: UNFORTUNATELY, THE COMPETITIVE SITUATION IS BECOMING INCREASINGLY DIFFICULT – AND THERE ARE SOME DAUNTING THREATS ON THE HORIZON.

Consider the following:

- There are likely upwards of 8,000 domestic competitors in express delivery in China today. And more are entering all the time, especially in intra-city delivery (i.e., deliveries within a single city).

- The cumulative market share of the top 4-5 express delivery companies has fallen from its previous 60-70% to less than 40-50%.

- Against this competitive picture, average prices have fallen +35% in the last 2-3 years (according to the State Post Bureau).

- At the same time, costs have been increasing, particularly labor which can be +40% of the cost structure.

- In cross-border delivery, the global giants (Fedex, DHL, TNT, UPS, etc.) are continuing to expand into China.

Overall, we see an increasingly difficult environment. There is increasing competition, falling prices, and rising costs - which is part of what is driving increasing capital requirements.

Plus, looming just on the horizon are some fairly daunting threats. For example, Lenovo has been rolling up some of the smaller delivery companies. Industrial and other Chinese giants (especially State-backed) have more than enough capital to enter this market.

And finally, there is Alibaba, Jingdong and the Internet e-commerce giants. As e-commerce surges, they have been moving into logistics and delivery from a position of strength. Alibaba's Cainiao (recently valued privately at $7.7B) now apparently has over 180,000 express delivery stations and 128 storage warehouses across China.

* * *

That's a bit of background. My goal with this article is to understand the recent acceleration by the market leaders in response to all this. Here's my conclusion:

Faced with this situation, the market leaders are racing for inter-city marketshare and operating scale.

First, a bit of competitive theory.

Keep in mind, most businesses have no real competitive advantages or barriers to entry. The leading companies do tend to get bigger and more efficient over time but they are never really protected from new entrants. And they are usually not particularly profitable, relative to capital. This very normal situation can be especially brutal in hyper-competitive China - as a trip to any electronics mart will show.

But in a small number of businesses, including express delivery, you can have powerful advantages that enable both long-term domination and profits (again relative to capital). You can see this type of domination in the financials of Fedex and UPS going back twenty years. There's a reason why Warren Buffett owns lots of UPS.

So faced with the above market and competitive picture, my question is: **Do China's express delivery majors have a viable path to such entrenched dominance? Can they become like Fedex?**

To answer this, it helps to view express delivery as three different businesses.

First, there is intra-city delivery, such as delivering packages from one office to another within, say, Shanghai. This is unbelievably competitive as pretty much anyone with a scooter can enter. Today, this business is a sea of private companies plus some lesser involvement by State-owned entities such as EMS. It is +50% of the overall market by volume and revenue. You can survive but you can't really win here.

Second, there is international / cross-border delivery. This market is more or less equally split between private Chinese companies, State-owned entities and the international delivery giants (Fedex, UPS, etc.). This business does offer the type of competitive advantages we are looking for. Unfortunately, the international giants are the ones that have them.

And third, there is cross-regional / inter-city service (i.e., sending from one part of China to another). This is the great hope of the Chinese express delivery leaders. Because inter-city delivery appears to offer the strong advantages we want. And I think this is what the recent acceleration and race to go public is really about. The majors are racing after this opportunity, and it requires lots of capital.

The goal is to get to an operational scale (i.e., trucks, warehouses, distribution centers, IT systems) that enables offering **rapid delivery to a national network of locations at prices others cannot match.**

That last part is the finish line. That's how you win. You offer national delivery at a price and speed your competitors can't match.

But to achieve this, you have to be larger than the other players. It is only when they have a size advantage (in volume and fixed costs) that you can actually price lower than your rivals (i.e., it's about economies of scale in the fixed costs of distribution relative to market size.). This is why the race for scale is so frantic. To win you don't just need to be big. You need to be bigger than the other guys.

I argue the key to winning in Chinese express delivery is getting to superior scale (both in volume and in operations) in cross-regional (not intra-city) delivery. At a minimum, this should result in some degree of protection from the increasing competition.

Ok. That was a bit of theory. I will go into more practical examples in the follow-up article. But I think this explains most of the actions we are seeing by China's express delivery companies - including:

- The race to go public (mostly by backdoor listings) and to raise capital.

- The rapid build out of operational scale (warehouses, distribution centers, trucks, etc.).
- The big investments in IT, automation and other geographically integrating assets.
- The launch of their own airlines. This part is pretty interesting.
- The increasing focus on cross-border delivery within Asia (but not beyond).

I do think this is the best strategy and it has worked elsewhere. But China is different and, ultimately, this approach may not be enough, especially against the e-commerce giants.

THE RUTHLESS BUT ENTERTAINING FIGHT TO BECOME THE "FEDEX OF CHINA" (PART 2)

By Jeffrey Towson

In the past year, SF Express, STO, YTO, and the other China express delivery giants have all hit the accelerator. Faced with mounting competitive threats, express delivery in the PRC has morphed into an arms race in capabilities and capital.

In Part 1, I explained what I think is behind the recent acceleration. In this part, I argue that 5 key actions will likely determine who will win - and become the "Fedex of China".

First, a quick summary of Part 1:

- Chinese express delivery is an awesome market. As good a China story as you will find.
- But there is increasing competition, falling prices, increasing operating costs and increasing capital requirements.
- Additionally, there are some daunting threats on the horizon, most notably the e-commerce and internet giants (Alibaba, etc.). They have been moving into logistics and delivery from a position of strength.
- Faced with this, China's express delivery giants are in a race to get to their most defensible position: superior marketshare and operational scale in cross-regional express delivery (i.e., delivery between cities). This, in theory, should enable **rapid delivery to a national network of locations - at prices and delivery times others cannot match.**

Based on this, I think five actions are going to largely determine which, if any, of the express delivery giants will win this race. The 5 actions are:

1: GO PUBLIC ASAP.

Most of the delivery giants have gone public - or have announced plans to do so. And they are trying to do this as fast as possible, frequently by reverse merger.

STO Express did a reverse merger by buying Zhejiang IDC Fluid Control. Alibaba-backed YTO Express is likely going to purchase garment company Dayang Group. ZTO has filed to list in the USA. And SF Express has just listed, a big reversal by founder Wang Wei on the whole idea of going public.

The goal is to get more capital ASAP. As mentioned in Part 1, the key to winning is not just to get big – but to be bigger than the others. So each competitor sees their rivals raising capital and doesn't want to fall behind.

2: BUILD OUT CROSS-REGIONAL OPERATIONS.

This raised cash will likely be used to build out operational platforms. This means lots of new warehouses, trucks, and distribution centers. This focus on cross-regional operations (i.e., deliveries between, not within, cities) is both about keeping up with the rapid market growth and trying to get bigger than rivals. They also might use the cash to buy market share, keep up with market growth and do some refinancing.

3: MAKE BIG INVESTMENTS IN IT, AUTOMATION AND OTHER GEOGRAPHICALLY INTEGRATING INTANGIBLE ASSETS.

The goal is to create operations that both enable lower pricing and that are difficult or expensive to replicate. Fixed assets like warehouses meet the first criteria but are not that expensive or difficult to replicate. Especially if competitors are utilizing a franchise model which requires less capital (an important factor in this).

However, IT and automation can accomplish both criteria in a powerful way. Automated distribution hubs increase productivity and decrease labor costs (a big deal in delivery). This can move the needle for overall delivery costs. Additionally, automated logistics are more difficult to replicate. It's no longer just a matter of spending money (i.e,. buying trucks and hiring staff).

4: LAUNCH AN OWNED AIRLINE.

Superior cross-regional operating scale (and capabilities) is about dropping costs and shortening delivery times across a national network of locations. Airplanes can have a big impact on this, especially for high volume routes. It's a critical part of the ultimate operating platform.

Several of the express delivery companies are already building their own airlines.

- SF Express launched an airline back in 2010. They now have about 37 planes.
- State-owned EMS operates an airline, albeit it in a more complicated SOE-type manner.
- YTO Express is launching an airline, initially to be based out of Hangzhou. They have five planes with 15 ordered and a plan for 50 planes by 2020.

Recall, Federal Express did express delivery via airplane from literally its first day of operations. In 1973, they began by flying 14 small planes carrying 186 packages to 25 US cities. They only later built out their ground operations. DHL was similar, beginning operations with an overnight air service in 1969.

This is a contrast to UPS, today the world's largest delivery company, which was originally a trucking company doing freight (they were founded before airplanes existed). They did not begin next-day-air until 1982. Similarly, TNT was launched in Australia in the 1940's with a single truck.

All the major Western express delivery companies eventually converged on each others' operating models (land plus air). So I expect to see a similar convergence in China, especially given its vast geography. A player without an airline will likely have increasing difficulty competing.

5: INCREASE CROSS-BORDER DELIVERY WITHIN ASIA - BUT PROBABLY NOT MUCH BEYOND.

Many of the leading China players are now expanding across Asia – offering express deliveries to Taiwan, Japan, Hong Kong and increasingly SE Asia. STO has its largest overseas logistics center in Hong Kong and can often deliver across Asia within 24 hours.

An Asia expansion makes sense for this strategy. But it raises the question of how international do you have to be to win in express delivery in China? Do you need to be global and offer delivery everywhere? Is Asia enough? Is Greater China enough?

Also keep in mind, international expansion puts the China companies in more direct competition with Fedex, DHL, and the others. This is a big deal. It means competing more with companies like UPS, which now delivers 18M pieces per day across 220 countries.

FINAL POINT: ALL OF THIS ULTIMATELY MAY NOT BE ENOUGH.

The race to become the "Fedex of China" is on and is increasingly frantic. Probably 2-3 of the big express delivery companies will get to this type of superior marketshare and operating scale. At that point, the more they can drop their unit costs via fixed costs, tangible fixed assets (airplanes, trucks, etc.) and intangible assets / capabilities (IT, automation, etc.) the more protected they will be.

However, it is not clear to me whether this will ultimately protect them from the e-commerce leaders moving downstream. Or from large Chinese industrials that want into this attractive market. All this may not be enough.

Ultimately, the "Fedex of China" may not end up being anything like Fedex.

STARBUCKS DOESN'T HAVE A SERIOUS COMPETITOR IN CHINA. IT'S WEIRD.

By Jeffrey Towson

Chinese Wanda is openly challenging Disney. Uber spent $2B fighting with Chinese DidiChuxing. Adidas has been fighting Chinese Li-Ning and Anta for decades. And Apple is now struggling against multiple rising Chinese competitors,(Xiaomi, Huawei, Oppo, etc.). One thing you can always count on in China: A successful international company will inspire serious domestic competitors.

So why doesn't Starbucks have a serious competitor in China? I've been asking people this for months and I still can't get a good answer. It's weird.

Starbucks has been in China since 1999 and currently has about 2,400 outlets. They have likely had the majority of the China retail coffee market for years. And CEO Howard Schultz has recently announced plans to open 500 new outlets per year. That will get them to 5,000 China stores by 2020.

Also, on Starbucks' November 3, 2016 earnings call, Schultz said "our newest class of Starbucks stores in China is delivering the highest AUVs, ROI and profitability of any store class in our history in the market."

So Starbucks in China has big market share, rapid growth and apparently attractive economics. Although they are breaking the #1 rule of doing business in China as a foreigner: If you are doing really well, keep it quiet.

Starbucks does have some smaller competitors in China. There is Costa Coffee from the UK. Costa is planning to have 900 China stores by 2020. There is CaffeeBebe from South Korea and Coffee Bean from Los Angeles. Both are fairly small in China. There is UBC Coffee (originally from Taiwan) but this is really more of a restaurant. And there is Pacific Coffee of Hong Kong, which has been majority acquired by China Resources.

You could also consider convenience stores like Family Mart and 7-11 as competitors. Certainly lots of coffee is sold there and they both have huge operational footprints. Also, there is McDonalds which has its McCafes. But these are a stretch as direct competitors I think.

Overall, I just can't point to any serious Chinese competitor for Starbucks. I don't see a China Mobile, Alibaba, Suning or Wanda-type company fighting them for their customers.

I've been asking around about this and here are the answers I have gotten so far:

EXPLANATION 1: STARBUCKS WAS THE FIRST MOVER AND THE MARKET WAS SLOW TO EMERGE.

Nestle entered China in 1990. Starbucks entered in 1999. But even as late as 2007 or so, it was not totally clear that Chinese consumers were going to drink coffee. I can remember being told over and over "You are waiguo. You don't understand China. We like tea, not coffee".

It took a long time for coffee to catch on in China. And even today coffee drinking is still somewhat rare. In 2013, the average Chinese consumed about 4 cups annually. That compares to 441 annually in the USA and over 1,000 cups in Norway (which I also don't understand.). Drinking coffee has been slow to develop in China thus far.

It also took a long time for Chinese consumers to rise enough in disposable income to afford Starbucks-type retail coffee. Even today, the prices in China (about 30rmb for a latte) are much more expensive than in the US on a purchasing power basis.

So Starbucks getting to the market first and having the long-term commitment to build in a slow-to-emerge market was important. Most companies were not prepared for such a long haul. This was not a rapid consumer success story, like we have seen with Pepsi, Tingyi, Apple and others.

EXPLANATION 2: STARBUCKS' BRAND AND SCALE GIVE THEM AN ADVANTAGE IN CRITICAL REAL ESTATE.

Winning in retail coffee hinges on getting the right locations. While customers are somewhat brand loyal, they generally won't walk five extra blocks to go to Starbucks if a Costa is across the street. Getting **high profile and high traffic locations** is critical.

Starbucks is now significantly larger than their competitors in many Chinese cities, which means they have more outlets, more customers and greater brand recognition. I think these scale advantages do give them an advantage in getting the best locations. They are probably offered the best locations (perhaps at a special price?) and can definitely outspend their smaller competitors on real estate because they have more cash, more customers and more brand power. They can open in the nice shopping mall rather than on the side street. They can be at the entrance of the mall rather than on the third floor. It's just much harder for a smaller company to acquire and afford these higher profile, higher traffic and higher price locations.

In theory, having the higher traffic and higher profile locations results in greater increases in sales and brand awareness – which then further increases their scale advantage. So it could be a virtuous cycle (in theory).

This explanation is that while the China coffee market looks big and fragmented, it is actually pretty consolidated when you map it out by the best locations in cities. Competing with Starbucks for these best spots is a lot harder than it appears.

EXPLANATION 3: SENIOR CHINESE BUSINESS HAVE A BLINDSPOT FOR COFFEE.

Even if all the above are true, I still don't see why coffee outlets could not be opened by a serious China competitor. There are over 160 Chinese cities with over 1M people. And this will increase to 220 cities by 2025. So even today, there is just a lot room for a new entrant, say in Chongqing or some other region.

What is really stopping a major company like China Resources from opening 500 stores? Why can't Wanda take over all the coffee outlets in their +100 Wanda Plazas? They are doing exactly that in hotels and cinemas at the moment. Why aren't the big boys of China entering this market?

Is it possible that the senior business people of China all grew up drinking tea and never really started drinking coffee? Maybe people like Wang Jianlin just don't like coffee?

This explanation would be consistent with the fact that the instant coffee market of China (probably +80% of the total coffee market) is +70% dominated by Nestle, another foreign company. Actually, come to think of it the energy drink market is also +80% dominated by RedBull. Maybe China' big business leaders just have a blind spot for caffeine?

FINAL EXPLANATION: IT COULD STILL BE A FAD.

This is the explanation that worries me. There is a possibility that retail coffee in China is, to some degree, a fad. Drinking expensive coffee with friends in a nice setting is still relatively new for most of China. This has only been going on for 5 years or so for most people. It is also sort of a status thing and Chinese consumers are notoriously fickle about what is currently cool. Is this somewhat a fad? Could the retail coffee market shrink by 20%? What if millennials lose interest? Could it ultimately be limited to just a small niche of the population? I think it is definitely possible. Maybe big companies are staying out because they don't really believe in it long-term.

*   *   *

The truth is I don't know why Starbucks doesn't have a serious competitor in China. Service businesses are an important new sector in China. And it is an area where local companies have struggled. Still, it seems very strange to me. Note: I am writing this in a Starbucks.

THREE WAYS CHINESE COMPANIES ARE WINNING WITH CUSTOMERS

By Jonathan Woetzel

Some of China's greatest successes have come in industries that require customer-focused innovation. Chinese firms are growing rapidly in such customer-facing sectors – such as household appliances (Chinese firms account for 39 percent of global revenue), Internet software (15 percent), and smartphones (over 10 percent and rising).

The advancement of Chinese companies in consumer-facing sectors is mostly driven by sales in local markets. Indeed, only in household appliances and consumer electronics do exports exceed 10 percent of sales. Largely based on the size of the Chinese consumer market, appliance makers such as Haier and Internet companies such as Baidu, Alibaba, and Tencent have become world leaders in their fields.

The success of Chinese companies in these industries illustrates some of the strengths that Chinese companies have in customer-focused innovation. Chief among these is the massive Chinese consumer market, as mentioned. China has become the world's largest market for smartphones, personal computers, air conditioners, refrigerators, microwaves, and home laundry appliances. Even niche markets in China, such as online gaming and beauty spas, are bigger than major industries such as autos in other economies.

However, the Chinese consumer market is not only large but also dynamic and fast-moving. Disposable income has risen by 10 percent per year in real terms over the past decade and, since 2000, more than 85 million households have joined the new mainstream consuming class (defined as households with disposable income of 106,000 to 229,000 RMB [$17,080 to $36,900]).

Some 106 million more households are expected to join the new mainstream consuming class by 2020. In this large and growing consumer market, innovations can be scaled up and commercialized rapidly. WeChat, a Chinese social media platform, garnered 100 million members in just 1.2 years—compared with 4.5 years for Facebook.

Chinese consumers also seem to be more willing than other consumers to participate in the innovation process by acting as perpetual beta testers. Consumer-facing companies routinely launch new models and continue to refine them based on market feedback. In 2014, for example, Xiaomi updated its smartphone operating system 52 times. Improving broadband and logistics networks also helps Internet content and retailing companies reach consumers efficiently.

Markets that rely on customer-focused innovation tend to have low barriers to entry, which is illustrated by the wave of Chinese entrepreneurs in Internet services, games, and e-commerce. In a 2013 job placement report, 12 percent of Peking University graduates said they had launched a company or were self-employed, compared to 4 percent in 2005. Venture investing has tripled, rising from $5.4 billion in 2010 to $16.9 billion in 2014.

Three things that Chinese companies are doing particularly well in terms of consumer-facing innovation are:

1. SOLVING CONSUMER PROBLEMS.

One of the biggest challenges facing Chinese consumers is the country's highly fragmented retail industry, which severely limits choice for consumers in all but the largest cities. Chinese entrepreneurs are building a world-leading e-commerce industry to address this problem.

From its start in 1999, Alibaba has grown into the world's largest online marketplace, based on the value of merchandise sold in its online stores ($394 billion in 2015. Alibaba's innovations include Alipay, a payments system, and Ali Finance, which provides financing for small-scale suppliers that are not served by the traditional banking system.

2. RETHINKING BUSINESS MODELS.

Nowhere have Chinese entrepreneurs shown a greater flair for innovation than in Internet-based businesses. In many cases, they have done so by inventing business models. For example, in most parts of the world, online businesses generate 60 to 90 percent of their revenue from advertising. However, in China, advertising is not as large a source of revenue—China's advertising industry is only about one-quarter the size of the US industry—and Chinese companies have been forced to create new business models to monetize web traffic. Tencent generates over 90 percent of its revenue from online games, sales of virtual items on social platforms, and e-commerce. Average revenue per user in 2014 was $16, $6 more than Facebook, according to 2014 annual reports.

YY.com, a video-based social communication platform, has built diverse revenue streams, including a virtual currency. In 2014, YY.com generated 56 percent of revenue from music and entertainment through sales of virtual goods such as virtual roses that viewers purchase to give to performers on the platform. Performers can redeem the virtual goods for cash and top performers can earn more than RMB 20,000 a month, seven times what the average factory worker earns.

3. FROM "GOOD ENOUGH" TO "CHEAPER AND BETTER."

For years, customer-focused innovation in China meant creating "good enough" products, which cost about half of what multinationals charged and delivered about 80 percent of the quality. Good enough products still work for lower-income consumers, but in an increasingly affluent China, innovators must create "cheaper and better" products to win new mainstream customers.

Xiaomi, a Beijing-based smartphone maker, became one of the world's most successful startups with products such as the Mi4. Xiaomi phones typically cost half as much as top-of-the-line products from other global brands, yet offered comparable or better hardware features. Business model innovations such as online only sales and risk sharing with suppliers helped Xiaomi offer its products at a low price. Xiaomi was the largest smartphone player (by shipments) in China, with more than 15 percent market share in 2015, and was entering foreign markets.

Since 2015 though new arrivals Oppo and Vivo have out-Xiaomi'd Xiaomi with cheaper models aimed at the rural and Tier 3/4 customers. These new rials are delivering through offline retail networks.

* * *

Over the past three decades, Chinese companies have learned to adapt products from around the world to the needs of a rapidly urbanizing nation and have become very agile—moving goods into production quickly, then tweaking designs afterward to better address consumer needs. A new generation of entrepreneurs is solving consumer problems and developing new business models, often in uniquely Chinese ways. Makers of consumer goods are changing their approaches to address the rising expectations of China's expanding middle class and moving beyond the "good enough" products of the past.

FINAL THOUGHTS

That's it for our four contrarian points. We hope this little book has been helpful to you – or at least a reasonable return on one hour (and $4).

We both post (and argue) online all the time. You can find us at LinkedIn and Twitter. Feel free to contact us or jump into any discussions we are having. Writing and publishing more and more seems to be about having these sorts ongoing discussions and communities online. And they're great fun, with lots of people chiming in from all over the world. Jeff also sends out a monthly "China recommended reading" email which you can sign up for at www.jeffreytowson.com.

Our last point is a thank you for reading. Both of us have published multiple books over the years but we have really changed our approach recently. We have shifted towards self-publishing and social media, both of which have been a blessing for writers. We have gained the ability to create without cost and to go direct to you. That's a real privilege and something we don't take for granted. Thanks again for taking the time to read this.

Cheers and best wishes from Shanghai and Beijing,

Jonathan and Jeff
June 2017

APPENDIX
OTHER CHINA STUFF TO KEEP AN EYE ON

We both try to keep an eye on new and emerging topics in China business. In fact, we teach a course on such emerging topics at Peking University. So we thought we would put in a couple here at the end. These are not contrarian positions but they are areas we are keeping an eye on. And we think they are pretty cool.

A GREAT MAP FOR UNDERSTANDING MODERN CHINA

By Jeffrey Towson

The "cluster" map shown below is originally by McKinsey & Co. I think it really illustrates three important points about modern China.

POINT 1: CHINA TODAY IS A SERIES OF CLUSTERS, NOT A CONTINENT.

China today is not yet an integrated continental economy. You don't see infrastructure seamlessly connecting each part of the country, like say in the United States and Europe. That is likely the future but not yet the present.

What you see today is a series of "clusters" - with each cluster containing 20-30 cities and typically over 60 million people. For example, Beijing / Tianjin in the North is actually a cluster of 28 cities – all increasingly interconnected by roads, rail and other new infrastructure. Qingdao, well known for its beer, is actually part of a 35-city cluster.

Chinese city clusters with average populations of 60M

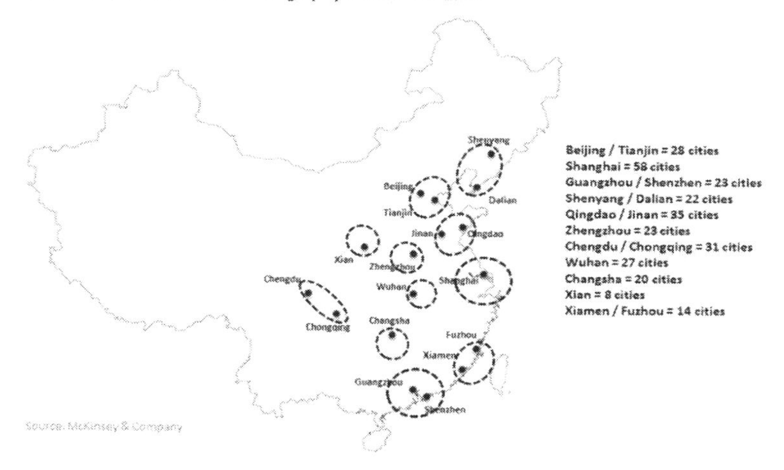

POINT 2: THESE +60M PERSON CLUSTERS ARE THE VAST MAJORITY OF THE ECONOMY.

China today has more than 20 of these clusters. Each is about the size of a large European country (more like France and Germany than Greece or Austria). According to government plans, China's main clusters will cover 80% of the GDP and 60% of the population.

POINT 3: URBANIZATION AND INFRASTRUCTURE ARE MOSTLY ABOUT BUILDING CLUSTERS.

Much of the highly publicized high-speed rail and other infrastructure projects are about creating clusters. It is about making it possible for people and goods to travel cheaply and quickly within a cluster. Some of the projects connect the clusters. The key metric to watch is the logistics cost within clusters, which has been falling fast.

GET READY FOR BEIJING THE +100M PERSON MEGA-CITY

By Jeffrey Towson

The emergence of Beijing as a +100M person mega-city is a pretty fascinating story. Some thoughts on where we are and what's coming next.

The economics of Beijing as a mega-city are already fantastic.

The population of the Beijing-Tianjin-Hebei cluster (also called "Jing-Jin-Ji") will be +100M people. And the economic output is already over 10% of China's GDP. So this is already a big deal in terms of people and money.

But it's going to get a lot bigger, especially given the new XiongAn suburban city project. By 2025, the Beijing the mega-city will be the world's fifth largest urban economy. At that point, it will be larger than London, Tokyo or New York.

PHASE I OF "BEIJING THE MEGA-CITY" WAS MOSTLY ABOUT INFRASTRUCTURE - AND THIS IS NOW LARGELY COMPLETE.

The Beijing-Tianjin-Hebei story thus far has been a story of infrastructure (i.e., lots of roads, rail, bridges). For example, Beijing's seventh ring road is now under construction and will extend the city directly into Hebei. The physical integration of Beijing-Tianjin-Hebei is largely complete. It is basically one gigantic, inter-connected mega-city.

But if Phase I was about building hardware, Phase II is going to be about the software. The story is going to shift from roads and trains to government policies, logistics, company operations, local services, family and culture, and so on. And this should be much more interesting.

PHASE II WILL ALSO BE ABOUT AN INCREASING CONCENTRATION OF FORTUNE 500 COMPANIES IN ONE PLACE.

Beijing already the most Fortune 500 headquarters and has +100 large company global headquarters. This is more than any other emerging market city, and sixth in the world (ahead of Seoul, Chicago and Los Angeles).

But as company concentration increases and as companies find it increasingly seamless to operate between Beijing, Tianjin and Hebei, the interactions between companies in Beijing should increase.

This is important. People are social animals. Putting so many top companies in close contact with each other will have lots of cumulative and synergistic effects. Think Hollywood, Wall Street, and Silicon Valley. Beijing is going to have a massive concentration of top companies - increasingly interacting with each other.

Phase II will also be about Beijing's huge and growing local consumer market.

The China consumer numbers are well-known. But it is worth repeating them quickly. By 2025, the Beijing the mega-city will have over 7 million households earning over US$20,000 per year. That will make it third or fourth on the global rich cities list. So this mega-city is going to be a massive consumer market in itself.

However, Phase II is also going to have big problems, including some we have not seen before.

We have never seen +100M person mega-cities. This is uncharted territory. Nobody really knows how these mega-cities are going to work. But for sure, there are going to be ongoing challenges for the local government to grapple with. This will include everything from how many police to have to what to do with all that sewage.

We are also going to see new types of problems. One example is the increasing number of migrant workers in Beijing. For Beijing, this could mean literally tens of millions of migrant workers living in the cities but outside the system. This is not a small problem. In Beijing, these migrants are sometimes referred to as “ant people”, because they frequently live underground in dormitories.

* * *

Ultimately, these mega-city clusters are the future of China. You can’t really build a >50 million person city as it becomes unworkable. Pollution, traffic, population, and housing pressures become increasingly problematic beyond a certain size. So creating hub-and-spoke systems around major cities (i.e., integrated mega-cities) like Beijing makes sense.

Now that the roads have been built, the real story of Beijing as a mega-city is just beginning. It should be fascinating to watch.

WANT REAL CHINA SOE REFORM? LET AB-INBEV AND THE CRAZY BRAZILIANS RUN SNOW BEER.

By Jeffrey Towson

AB-InBev has closed their $104B mega-acquisition of SABMiller. As part of this, they agreed to sell SAB's 49% stake in Snow beer . This was a preemptive move to get Chinese regulatory approval. As a result, quasi-SOE CR Snow will now become 100% state-owned (by China Resources Enterprise).

This is a real shame.

Because lost in the media coverage of this huge beer deal is the fact that we almost had AB-InBev running CR Snow. We almost had the world's most aggressive management meritocracy taking charge of a big Chinese SOE (mostly). This would have been Chinese SOE reform like nobody has ever seen before.

Here's my take on what I think would have happened (and I'm hoping still might somehow).

STEP 1: THE BRAZILIANS THAT RUN AB-INBEV (AND 3G CAPITAL) DESCEND ON CR SNOW LIKE THE SPARTANS OF THE MOVIE 300.

The movie 300 is a good analogy for the management philosophy of this hyper-aggressive group of Brazilian businessmen. For those who haven't seen the movie, it's the violent and frequently slow motion story of 300 mostly naked Spartan warriors taking on the entire Persian army. The Spartans were famous for having been trained to fight since birth. And for their extreme aggression. They were the uber-warriors of ancient Greece.

That's a good way to think about the management-style pioneered by 3G's founders (Jorge Lemann, Carlos Sicupira, and Marcel Telles). They are the Spartans of management. They are famous for taking over companies in Brazil, Europe and the US - and then turning them into hyper-competitive meritocracies.

For example, in 2004 they merged their Brazilian company Ambev with Belgian Interbrew. They basically combined the world's 3rd and 5th largest beer companies. Post-deal, their Brazilian managers descended on the traditional culture at the Belgian HQ like the Spartans. Within two years, profits had jumped $0.9B to $2.2B.

In 2008, they bought the world's largest beer maker Anheuser-Busch for $52B (using a lot of debt). They quickly cut over $1B in costs, fired or encouraged 1,400 employees to leave and got rid of $9B of assets. Profits jumped.

But their primary tool is not cost cutting. It is the cultural transformation of management. They take-over and turn the management into crazy Spartans like themselves. And they openly want "crazy" people. According to Sicupira, "It's easier to rein in a guy who's crazy than push someone who is slow."

STEP 2: THEY WOULD IMPLEMENT A NEW TYPE OF CHINESE SOE REFORM.

The 3G playbook is now fairly well known, especially for beer companies. We would likely see three major initiatives at CR Snow:

#1 - Introduction of meritocracy plus partnership

They change management compensation so it has low salaries and huge performance bonuses. And performance is then strictly measured. This creates a meritocracy where you rise and fall based on performance alone. In fact, the founders don't allow any of their +10 children (and increasing number of grandchildren) to work at any of their companies - as this would undermine the culture of meritocracy.

They then pair meritocracy with partnership (i.e,. ownership). At Anheuser-Busch, they gave 39 senior executives a package of 28M share options. But these were given as an all-or-nothing reward based on reducing the company's debt by half in about 5 years. If the team had failed in this, they would have gotten nothing. But when they succeeded two years early they received $1B in bonuses (yes, $1 billion to 39 people). You can see why this sort of pay structure would attract Spartan-like personalities.

#2 - Righteous and ongoing cost-cutting.

This is what gets 3G in the news regularly. They are famous for their extreme cost cutting and for implementing zero-based budgeting (the yearly budget starts out a zero and each cost must be argued up from zero. This breaks spending by habit). It is routine for them to immediately take away all the private offices, the company cars, the secretaries, the jets and business class air tickets, etc. They cut everything they can and the cutting never stops.

For example, at Anheuser-Busch, they sold the fleet of planes and everyone now flies coach. They ended free distribution of beer and free tickets to St. Louis Cardinals games. As mentioned, they decreased the workforce by 1,400. They even dropped the number of blackberries used by staff from 1,200 to 720.

#3 - Cultural change

Ultimately their biggest tool is cultural change. They are the Spartans. They transform the culture by bringing in their own people and by driving out those who won't adapt to their style.

The most famous example of this was during an early Brazilian takeover (recounted in the book *Dream Big*). The story goes that approximately 35 executives of a recently taken-over company met with Sicupira to complain about the new compensation system.

They then went to lunch. While they were out eating, he had them fired and locked out.

Ultimately, their Spartan management system is based on creating a team of fanatics and giving them a way to get rich through longer-term profit performance.

STEP 3: THEY WOULD GUIDE CR SNOW TO INCREASING SCALE AND DOMINANCE IN CHINA.

There is enough history of 3G's approach to conclude it would work at a Chinese SOE. They pioneered this in Brazil in the 1990's, when many companies were bureaucratic and state protected. Their strategy (both by take-over and PE) was to invest in undervalued companies and give them the Spartan shock treatment.

However, it wasn't clear back then whether this shock therapy would work on European or American companies. That question has now been answered. See the financial performance of Interbrew, Anheuser-Busch, Heinz, and Burger King. It turns out successful Western companies (especially when run by the founders' heirs) can also grow lazy and bloated over time.

CR Snow is now the largest brewer in China. But at 30% marketshare they are not truly dominant yet. I think 3G would rapidly grow CR Snow to dominance in China - and probably Asia.

* * *

A couple final comments on this. I teach 3G's strategy at Peking University. My take is that it can be incredibly effective in specific situations. Such as:

- When it is a big company with lots of bloat to cut. This type of bloat frequently accumulates in big successful companies over time.

- When there are multiple internal operating entities that can be made to compete and share best practices. 3G did this with restaurant franchises at Burger King, with manufacturing facilities at Heinz (and others) and with breweries at several beer companies. Cost cutting gets you benefits but it is the long-term productivity gains that really matter most.

- When the business is one where you can cut costs without impacting quality significantly. Cutting costs aggressively in beer is likely not going to impact beer quality. But cutting costs this way in hospitals can impact quality very easily. Simple products work better for this approach.

- The business can grow just by doing more of the same. 3G doesn't really do innovation, technology or product development. They expand by doing more of what they are already doing - like by selling more beer or ketchup.

Overall, the 3G approach works best on companies that don't require innovation, product development or advanced brainpower. They want businesses with proven branded products or services where you can cut costs, drive productivity and expand existing sales.

A final comment.

SOE reform is arguably one of the biggest drivers of real GDP growth in China. It has had a huge impact thus far and is an important area going forward.

But consider how tepid SOE reform has been in recent years. Now compare that to the Spartan management style I have just described. That contrast is China's lost opportunity in this beer mega-merger. 3G taking over CR Snow would be a real sight to see.

HOW ORIENTAL DREAMWORKS AND "CREATIVE CHINA" ARE DISRUPTING HOLLYWOOD.

By Jeffrey Towson

China is inching closer to becoming the world's largest entertainment market and Hollywood studios are struggling to adapt.

Cameos by Chinese film stars are being jammed, often nonsensically, into Western movies. Studio executives are flying in to meet with cash-rich Chinese moguls. And praise for China in Hollywood films has become commonplace. This is increasingly being described as self-censorship. I tend to use the word "slobbering".

But the China phenomenon that could impact Hollywood the most is not the "big money" or the "big market" stories that are now so common. It is the millions of artists, animators and other creative professionals who are now emerging in China. Of the 19M students in Chinese universities in 2009, over 1M were studying art and design, more than the students in science, law, education, or economics. And this wave of creative talent is now entering the workforce in droves.

We are witnessing the rise of a huge new creative class in China - literally millions of artists, designers, animators and other creative professionals are entering the workforce. Oriental DreamWorks (ODW) in Shanghai is at the forefront of this new "creative China" - and may end up being its midwife.

Earlier this year, the Oriental DreamWorks' co-produced film "Kung Fu Panda 3" was released in China and set a new record as the top-grossing animated movie. It's a good indication of what is to come: world-class animated movies made mostly by Chinese talent and with Chinese characteristics.

ARTIST COLONIES, NOT BUSINESS UNITS.

Oriental DreamWorks was launched in 2012 by company chiefs Jeffrey Katzenberg and Li Ruigang. Today, it has a creative team of about 150 artists and animators based in Shanghai. And 90% of these artists are native Chinese, most trained in local art and design schools. The staff overseeing project development are roughly an equal mix of native Chinese and Chinese-Americans with Hollywood experience. This "best of both worlds" team structure and Oriental DreamWorks creative chief Peilin Chou are good examples of what "creative China" will likely look like.

We are starting to see large numbers of domestically trained artists working with creative teams with both Hollywood and China experience. And while it is tempting to think of these teams as business units, in practice they function more like artist colonies. The process is fluid and creative. Success comes from a mix of talent, process and culture. And given the sheer volume of Chinese talent emerging, there will likely be thousands of these creative teams soon. They are going to produce a ton of content. For example, during the National Day holiday week in October 2016 alone, seven new animated movies were released into Chinese theaters.

According to Peilin Chou, "There is just a tremendous amount of talent here. I would say the biggest difference between artists here and artists that have worked on major Hollywood films is not lack of talent or lack of drive or ambition. It's just that that they haven't had the opportunity yet to work on world-class quality animated films until now."

And in a nice bit of karma, Hollywood's relatively few Asian-Americans have become increasingly critical for the industry's China ambitions. It turns out making films that resonate strongly with Chinese families requires actual experience in Chinese families, or at least in the culture or language.

Chou is a good symbol for this. Born in Taiwan and raised in northern California, she graduated from the University of California Los Angeles' communications department the same year that Katzenberg, then head of Walt Disney Studios, launched an internship program to bring minorities into the studio system. That first year's crop of interns included Chou, who was placed at Touchstone Pictures, and Leo Chu, who ended up at what is now Walt Disney Animation Studios. The two soon discovered they were just about the only Asian-Americans executives in Hollywood.

Chou recalls her first meeting of Coalition of Asian Pacifics in Entertainment (CAPE), an industry advocacy group. "There were maybe a dozen of us at most, and most were assistants," she said. "CAPE just celebrated its 25th anniversary this year with a gala event filled with hundreds. It's so gratifying and exciting to see."

Over the following decades, Chou worked in development at Touchstone Pictures and Walt Disney Animation as well as at several television networks (Spike TV, Nickelodeon, AZEAN TV) and on Broadway theater productions. She was also one of the executives responsible for overseeing the Walt Disney film "Mulan," the first animated movie based on a Chinese character. Around the same time, she was also lobbying her studio to hire a then-unknown Taiwanese director named Ang Lee.

Twenty years later, Katzenberg would ask Chou to come to Shanghai to oversee creative development at Oriental DreamWorks, making her one of a select group of executives who have run creative development at both Hollywood and Chinese studios. Indeed, the few Asian-Americans in Hollywood with development experience now find themselves in great demand as studios struggle with how to appeal to Chinese viewers.

"The studio system in L.A. today is very different than when my career started," Chou said. "Hollywood now is pretty exclusively focused on tentpole films and superhero movies, star actor or director vehicles. The more modestly budgeted romantic comedies, for example, are not really part of the game anymore. In China, the opposite is true. Every year, more and more movies are getting made. People are taking chances, and it's really exciting to be a part of an industry that's growing and expanding, and have the opportunity to be part of a culture that is still development-driven by great ideas and stories first."

GET READY FOR ENTERTAINMENT HYPER-COMPETITION

Millions of Chinese artists and animators means lots more movies and TV shows. It also means things are probably going to happen cheaper and faster. Studios in China can simply deploy far more artists than they can in Hollywood.

For top quality films this probably won't make much difference. Per Warren Buffett, you can't make a baby in one month by getting nine women pregnant. But for lower quality films and TV shows, the Chinese entertainment market is probably going to surge in volume. And it is going get a lot faster and more ruthless.

I suspect we are at the end of what has been Hollywood's golden age in China. A period when Chinese consumers had money and flocked to theaters to see the latest films, but when serious Chinese competitors have not yet arrived. However, this will happen soon, just as it has for so many other industries. As Chinese studios increase their production quantity and quality, they are likely going to wipe out (or at least challenge) much of Hollywood's current success in China.

In practice,"mass creativity" in China will mean lots more creative teams, operating at a lower cost base than Hollywood and fighting far greater domestic competition. Creative China is going to be a larger, faster and more ruthless industry than its U.S. counterpart. ODW is in good shape for this fight. But I suspect Hollywood studios that haven't built their own operations in the Mainland will be in trouble. Stay tuned.

(originally published in Nikkei Asian Review, here, reprinted with permission)

CHINA'S DRUG AND VACCINE SCANDALS WILL DWARF ITS FOOD SCANDALS

By Jeffrey Towson

It was the 2008 melamine baby powder scandal that finally made food safety a national priority in China. And the 2016 vaccine scandal may be what similarly finally wakes Chinese consumers up to the issue of drug safety. Unfortunately, sick newborns may again be the mobilizing image.

Drug scandals have been happening in China for a long time. But they have mostly been below the media radar. As recently as late 2015, the US FDA banned 15 drug products from Pfizer-partner Zhejiang Hisun. Their cited concern was quality controls at the

China facilities. Hisun has since said it has addressed the problems. But this example is particularly concerning because Hisun is arguably the best of the +700 Chinese facilities involved in drug making today.

So if Hisun had issues it raises the question: **How big of a problem is drug safety in China?**

My prediction is that drug scandals will eventually dwarf the food scandals in terms of morbidity, mortality and reach. Here is my argument:

#1 DRUG SCANDALS CAUSE GREATER MORBIDITY AND MORTALITY THAN FOOD SCANDALS BECAUSE THEY HIT MORE VULNERABLE POPULATIONS.

The melamine milk powder scandal was a turning point because it impacted a particularly vulnerable population (i.e., newborns). But pharmaceuticals are regularly consumed by other highly vulnerable populations. In particular, the sick and the elderly.

For example, in 2012, Chinese authorities detained approximately 2,000 people in a crackdown on fake and counterfeit drugs. The fake drugs they seized included those used to treat cancer, hypertension and diabetes. What was the likely impact of these fake drugs on cancer patients? Or of the long-term use of fake hypertension and diabetes drugs by those with chronic conditions?

The human cost of fake, contaminated and substandard drugs on the sick and elderly is simply much greater than that of food scandals.

#2 DRUG SCANDALS ARE HARDER TO DETECT.

Food scandals are actually relatively easy to catch. The food tastes or looks funny. Healthy people feel sick and go to the ER. Plus you can just walk into a food processing plant or restaurant and catch things like workers using old meat.

But fake, contaminated and substandard pharmaceuticals (or their ingredients) are hard to detect. A pill looks like a pill. And patients rarely become acutely ill (many are already sick anyways). You usually need specialized equipment to check the quality of the pills.

Note that in the recent vaccine scandal, in which vaccines were likely sold after their expiration dates, there were no real visible outcomes. If the ring hadn't been caught, the parents would likely have never known that their children weren't actually immunized.

Drug scandals are a much harder problem to detect, even when you are actively looking for it.

#3 THE FAKE DRUG INDUSTRY IS BIG AND PROFITABLE.

The fake drug industry has been around for a long time. Companies sell everything from fake Viagra to diluted hypertensives. They also sell drugs that have been banned in the West for safety reasons. And all of this is big money. The couple in the recent vaccine scandal had over $90M in illegal sales.

Plus there are hundreds, if not thousands, of these mostly fly-by-night companies. They sell into the supply chain, via little retail stores, in backdoor pharmacies and on the Internet. In 2013 alone, Chinese police closed down 140 illegal websites and online pharmacies in 29 provinces. It's a problem that is both profitable and difficult to stop.

#4 UNLIKE MOST FOOD SCANDALS, DRUG SCANDALS ARE A GLOBAL PROBLEM.

If you are taking a pill in the US, part of it probably came from China. Over 80% of the world's active pharmaceutical ingredients are now made in China and India (but mostly in China). So these drug problems have global reach.

The most famous example of this was the 2008 Heparin scandal. Tainted Heparin from China ended up killing over 240 Americans. As a result, 34 China facilities (via Baxter International) were banned from exporting.

And it gets more complicated. A lot of these quality problems are actually in the chemistry, as opposed to just in the final drug or in the active pharmaceutical ingredient. In 2012, police in China detained +60 people who were making chromium-tainted gel capsules with industrial waste. The police seized over 77 million gel capsules and shut down 80 production lines. Think about those numbers for a moment. 77M capsules and 80 production lines.

But the biggest "global" aspect of this problem is likely in other developing economies. Fake drugs are everywhere in SE Asia and Africa. And many are coming from China. The morbidity and mortality resulting from this is hard to overstate. For example, the Wellcome Trust estimated that one-third of the malaria drugs in Uganda may be fake or substandard.

Final Point: Pharmaceuticals in China are going to grow. But absent improvements, drug scandals could also become much bigger as well.

Healthcare spending today in China is about 6% of GDP, up from 4-5% a few years ago. It is likely on its way to 12-13%. And China's pharmaceutical market, already big at $108B (2015), is growing along with this. All of this is good news. It follows naturally from growing domestic demand (aging + increasing wealth + more chronic disease) and a continued movement of pharmaceutical production to China.

So this is a big market that is growing fast and developing in sophistication. But it logically follows that any future quality problems will also be larger in scale. That is worrisome.

BASEBALL IS COPYING THE NBA IN CHINA AND IT MIGHT WORK.

By Jeffrey Towson

These are boom times for sports in China. An increased national focus on health and fitness is coinciding with a big increase in entertainment consumption. And the State Council has set a goal of making the sports industry a 5 trillion yuan ($750 billion) sector by 2025.

So stadiums and fields are being built, European soccer teams are being purchased and Adidas is opening stores as fast as possible. Sportswear has even become the fashionable attire in China.

Against this backdrop, baseball is playing a long game to become a major spectator sport in China. And while America's favorite pastime has long been all but ignored in the world's most populous nation, this may finally be changing. Major League Baseball, the U.S. professional league, has been quietly and patiently making all the right moves in China.

The National Basketball Association is really the model for sports success in China. It is wildly popular, with over 30 million regular weekly viewers and more than 200 million tuning in for big games. Even President Xi Jinping has said he watches the NBA in his spare time. How basketball went from a mostly local activity to mass-market entertainment in China is an important business story.

The NBA's success is frequently attributed to retired Chinese star Yao Ming. This is mostly incorrect. Certainly Yao was a unique phenomenon who catapulted the sport upwards but the NBA had already been in China for over 15 years before Yao joined the Houston Rockets in 2002. Michael Jordan, the Chicago Bulls and the Olympic "Dream Team" were already well known in China by that time.

The NBA's success in China has actually been more about a clever long-term business strategy, which is what MLB appears to be replicating.

DRAWING VIEWERS

The NBA has long provided free public access to its games in China. Starting in 1987 state broadcaster China Central Television began showing weekly game highlights that the NBA sent on video tapes to Beijing. This was particularly good timing as CCTV then had little competition for viewers and Michael Jordan was becoming a big draw. The NBA has continued to provide free access since, most recently via a deal for online streaming with Tencent Holdings.

MLB has put in place a similar free mass dissemination strategy. Since around 2008, MLB games have been shown on more than 10 government TV channels, reaching most of the population. Under a three-year deal signed in January, Le Sports, an affiliate of online streaming company Leshi Internet Information & Technology, is streaming 125 live games in China per season.

These are the early moves in a long-term strategy. The Chinese Baseball Association was only formed in 2002 and MLB did not have a China office until 2007. According to Leon Xie, managing director of MLB China, there were then only three real baseball diamonds in all of China.

MLB is very unlikely to create a phenomenon as big as Yao Ming but it is working to develop Chinese players. MLB opened its first training camp in the country in 2009, in the eastern city of Wuxi. Training centers have also opened in Changzhou and Nanjing. Some younger players have gone to the U.S. to play in elite high school leagues. In 2015, Xu Guiyuan became the first player trained in Wuxi to sign with an MLB club, joining the Baltimore Orioles.

Players at the training centers are now playing over 100 games a year and often moving directly onto Chinese university baseball teams upon graduation. The number of baseball diamonds in China has grown to over 50. And the official Chinese Baseball League, which had gone dormant, was relaunched in 2014 in partnership with property developer Hengda Lianghe Investment.

As shown by the success of the NBA's Jeremy Lin, Chinese consumers can also become very enthusiastic about Asian-American athletes. Given that baseball is popular in the U.S. and Taiwan, these could be sources for high-profile ethnic Chinese players. For example, Chinese-American Ray Chang, born in Kansas City, has been playing for minor league teams for more than a decade and is now on a team affiliated with the Cincinnati Reds.

FOCUS ON EYEBALLS

Ultimately, it wasn't getting lots of people to play basketball that made the NBA wildly successful in China and it wasn't building basketball courts. The key was getting hundreds of millions of Chinese to become big fans.

Basketball and the NBA is more something that is watched on television. People play but far more people watch. And by around 2005, the NBA had become an almost one-of-a-kind cross-border media vehicle. Between Yao Ming and years of free games on CCTV, the league had captured a large viewership. As a result, large Chinese and Western companies began seeing the NBA games as a way to reach Chinese consumers. They began placing Chinese-language ads in places like the Houston Rockets' arena.

Western multinationals like Nike and McDonald's also began partnering with the NBA as a way to expand their business in China. Walking into a KFC or McDonald's outlet in China, you will often see NBA promotions. Nike funded basketball camps for teens. Many large companies became deeply invested in the success of the NBA in China.

Building this type of media platform and corporate "team approach" was a big part of the NBA's success. This will be one of the big challenges for MLB in China.

MLB is going to have to follow a long-term strategy. It will be a process of introducing baseball as media entertainment and building a following. It will likely take decades, not years. MLB held its first game in China just nine years ago, about 30 years after the NBA's local debut. But unlike virtually every other industry in China, entering late in sports is not necessarily a disadvantage.

Baseball is the third-largest sport globally, with 10% of the market by value and a high concentration in East Asia. MLB's 30 teams produced $10 billion in revenue in 2015. Since entering China almost a decade ago, the league has slowly been making smart moves. Baseball could be a surprise hit in China.

Article re-posted from Asian Nikkei Review (here). Reprinted with permission.

HOW CHINA'S "PUFF DADDIES" BECAME THE WORLD'S BIGGEST SMOKERS (PROBABLY)

By Jeffrey Towson

What do you get when you put the 650M Chinese men who are the world's biggest smokers in the China's most polluted cities? And then wait for +20 years?

You get approximately 20M super-smoking men. A group that has likely inhaled more carcinogens than any other human beings alive. I call this group of men China's "puff daddies".

Here's my little calculation on this.

- China is a huge smoking country. There are 350M smokers and China produces over 40% of the world's cigarettes.
- But if you take the top 20% of these smokers (by consumption), you get about 60-70M really heavily smoking people. These are the really high-powered, 1-2 packs a day smokers.
- And if you take the 20% of those that live in the most polluted cities (assuming an even geographic distribution), that gets you about 15-20M Chinese super-smokers.
- And as only 4% of Chinese smokers are women, these +20M "super-smoking meets super pollution-inhaling Chinese" are almost all guys.

These +20M Chinese "puff daddies" are an interesting demographic to watch. They will inhale more pollutants in their lifetimes than probably any other group alive. And it is a pretty big group. It is as if the entire population of Australia was replaced by super-smoking men. And, unfortunately, as time goes by their medical conditions are going to become more and more apparent.

China's puff daddies are really five factors playing out in combination:

FACTOR 1: CHINA HAS VERY HIGH PREVALENCE OF SMOKING AND A VERY LARGE POPULATION.

The China smoking numbers are well-known: 300-350M smokers consuming 130 billion packs of cigarettes per year. This is about a third of the world's cigarettes annually. It results in 1.3M deaths per year (about 10% of all deaths in China).

It is very unusual to have such a big population with such a high smoking prevalence. Greece is actually #1 for smoking per capita. But China is far and away #1 in the aggregate.

FACTOR 2: CHINA'S AIR QUALITY IS A MAJOR HEALTH THREAT - AND THIS IS LIKELY SYNERGISTIC WITH SMOKING.

Air pollution is more of a Northern China phenomenon, as that's where a lot of the polluting factories are. In Beijing, where I live, the air quality index (AQI) typically goes between 50 and 250. At 100, I usually start to wear a mask. At 200 (described as "very unhealthy" on my phone app), school kids are kept indoors. And on the "airmageddon" days (300-400 and above), things start to shut down. It's like walking in fog.

Most studies argue that pollution is now the 4th biggest health threat in China, behind heart disease, dietary risk and, yes, smoking. And smoking, unfortunately, can have a synergistic effect when combined with other inhaled carcinogens (i.e., the cancer rates go up more in combination with some pollutants).

FACTOR 3: SECOND-HAND SMOKE IS A PROBLEM IN A DENSE COUNTRY WITH A SMOKING CULTURE.

Second-hand smoke is also a big deal in China. Lots of people smoking impacts other people. Volume, density and social acceptability matter. According to PRC researchers, over 700 million Chinese are affected by secondhand smoking.

And unfortunately, this has a particularly cumulative effect when it happens indoors - such as in restaurants, offices, bars and homes. According to the WHO, the air in a restaurant with three smokers reaches a 600 AQI level. And it increases to 1,200 with five smokers.

The irony here is that when the pollution is really bad outside, everyone tends to stay inside, where they then smoke in close quarters.

FACTOR 4: LUNG CANCER SURVIVAL RATES ARE LOW.

The 5 year lung cancer survival rate is very low. This depends on the type and the stage of the cancer, but even Stage 1 non-small cell cancer (arguably the best kind) has only a 50% five-year survival rate. According to the American Lung Association, the five year survival rate for lung cancer overall is about 17%.

This is not a disease that most people survive. China's puff daddies are looking like a very high mortality demographic.

FACTOR 5: SMOKING IS NOT REALLY DECREASING MUCH IN CHINA.

The percentage of the Chinese population that smokes has been holding steady at about 24% - but the population itself is still growing. So the total number of Chinese smokers is still increasing overall. Although smoking by Chinese women is decreasing.

Additionally, the average number of cigarettes consumed daily per smoker has actually increased (according to JAMA). The average Chinese smoker consumed about 15 cigarettes a day in 1980. In 2012, it had risen to 22. So this is increasing as well.

* * *

Overall, China's puff daddies are the result of a unique combination of China factors. And unfortunately, in the next decade, we can probably expect to see a bow wave of lung cancer from this. China's puff daddies, arguably the world's biggest smokers, will be riding the top of this wave.

Thanks to Vijay Vaitheeswaran for suggesting the name puff daddies.

WHY DID APPLE INVEST IN DIDI? BECAUSE THAT'S HOW BIG COMPANIES START DATING

By Jeffrey Towson

There was a lot of discussion about the rationale for Apple's 2016 $1B investment in Chinese DidiChuxing. Why did they do it? Will it garner goodwill with the Chinese government? Will it help Apple's slowing sales in China? And so on.

My answer to all of these questions is no. I don't think the deal has any immediate implications for Apple or Didi. And I don't think it has any super big business rationale either.

That doesn't mean it's a bad deal. In fact, It looks pretty smart. But it appears mostly to be about building a relationship. I think Apple CEO Tim Cook and Didi President Jean Liu recognized that they have complementary expertise and share a common future in China (and technology). So this simple, limited-risk deal was a way to begin a relationship – and to access expertise. Minority investments are how big companies start to date each other.

My take is four points:

#1: THIS IS NOT GOING TO GARNER MUCH GOODWILL WITH THE CHINESE GOVERNMENT.

This appears to be the New York Times' main explanation for the deal. But Chinese total M&A for 2015 was $735B and outbound M&A was about $60B (PwC). A lack of capital is not a huge concern of the Chinese government today, as compared to 1995. And $1B barely registers.

Plus, Didi has a complicated government situation. Yes, local governments like the potential impact of ride-sharing on congestion but they are also against excessive disruption of State-owned taxi companies. They are also against making lots of taxi drivers angry. Similarly, provincial governments may be supportive but maybe not if ride sharing decreases demand for cars (auto manufacturing, servicing, auto parts suppliers). Keep in mind, the auto sector creates huge employment and the major car companies are significantly State-owned.

So is putting $1B cash into an already complicated political situation an obvious win for Apple's government relations in China? I don't think so. If Apple really wants to improve its relations with China's government then their deals will need to include words like "new R&D center" and "technology transfer".

#2: THIS DEAL IS NOT GOING TO GROW APPLE'S BUSINESS IN CHINA ANYTIME SOON.

This seems to be Bloomberg's take. Apple's business in China is selling iPhones and iPads. Will a passive minority investment in a transportation app funding round change this? Does it change the competitive dynamic with Samsung or Xiaomi? It doesn't.

Additionally, there are arguments (WSJ here) that the deal could increase acceptance of Apple Pay in China. But against truly dominant competitors like Tenpay and Alipay? Getting Apple Pay on more phones is good. But competing against these entrenched local giants is the real challenge.

#3:THIS DEAL IS NOT A BIG FINANCIAL INVESTMENT FOR APPLE.

This is a tiny investment for Apple given their $233B cash balance (3Q2016). It could turn out to give good returns (note: Didi's 2016 private market price was $25B. Up from $6B in February 2015). And perhaps Apple is benefiting from using foreign money that would be taxed if repatriated to the US.

But it's just not a big enough investment to move the needle for Apple. And Apple is not a financial investor anyways. They typically acquire smaller tech companies in order to absorb them. So why are they participating in a funding round for a Chinese start-up anyways?

#4: THIS DEAL ALSO HAS NO MAJOR IMPACT ON DIDI.

$1B will also not change much for Didi. They raised $3B in a few months in 2015 and can probably raise significant capital anytime they want in China. So yes, cash is certainly a strength but it is a strength that Didi already has.

The big question for Didi in this deal is technology, the one area where Uber claims (and probably has) an advantage. This is not technology at the app and coding level but in the bigger trends coming like self-driving cars. Uber is well positioned to integrate its service into other leading Western car, transportation and technology companies. And Apple is widely rumored to be investing heavily in auto technology (self-driving? electric?). A technology gap is probably a concern for Didi.

So a key question is "is Apple bringing something that impacts the technology capabilities of Didi?" The answer appears to be "not yet". It looks like a pure financial investment right now. But maybe there are data or technology sharing aspects to the deal that have not been disclosed? Or maybe it will happen down the road? And that is my main point. Apple and Didi share a common future in technology and China.

So why did they do the deal? Well, because they like each other and this starts a relationship.

Sometimes M&A it not about the strategy or synergies or returns. Sometimes it is about the individual personalities (Did Jack Ma really buy Evergrande Football Club because it helps Alibaba?). Sometimes people do deals just to do them. And because of the relationships. M&A is ultimately person-to-person.

So why did they do the deal?

Honestly, I think Jean and Tim met. I think they liked each other and they liked each others' companies. And they had already recognized the value of each others' expertise and experience. It is reported that Apple and Didi had been in communication for a year prior to the deal.

Long-term, Apple needs China and Didi needs technology. They have complementary expertise and share a common future in China and technology. So they just did a simple, no-risk deal. And in doing so, they created a more formal relationship between their two companies. I don't see much business rationale beyond that. They went from flirting to dating - but they haven't yet married (a strategic partnership, a joint venture, etc.)

And perhaps this initial deal is just the first step toward larger collaborations? Perhaps a joint venture in cars? Large deals do tend to follow smaller ones.

Perhaps this relationship will turn out to be critical for one of them at a later time? A financial back-stop? It's usually best to build your bridges before you need them.

Or perhaps they are just two leading tech CEOs who recognize the world is changing quickly (the rise of China; the collision of technology, cars and transportation; the rapid emergence of more Chinese smartphone makers, etc). So working together on a changing terrain is a smart move in general.

I would be on the look-out for a potential big deal to follow this initial smaller one. What comes next with Apple and Didi will be interesting to watch.

10012589R00143

Printed in Germany
by Amazon Distribution
GmbH, Leipzig